A Brief History of the Sacraments:
Baptism and Communion

Robert C. Jones

Robert Jones
POB 1775
Kennesaw, GA 30156

robertcjones@mindspring.com

First Edition

ISBN: 1450566928
EAN-13: 9781450566926

This book is dedicated to the members of the Christian History and Theology Sunday School class at Mars Hill Presbyterian Church, Acworth, GA

Table of Contents

Introduction

Since the time of the Reformation, most of Protestantism has celebrated two sacraments - "baptism and supper". And while the Roman Catholic church and the Eastern Orthodox church celebrate five more[1], almost all Christians celebrate baptism and communion.

This book will provide a brief history into the practice of those two sacraments, and show how those practices diverged over time between denominations. Part One discusses the celebration of the Lord's Supper (also known as the Eucharist, Communion, etc.) Part Two will discuss baptism, and provides a chapter on the question of "Infant verses Believers' Baptism".

An appendix discusses the question of whether the baptism practiced by John the Baptist might have had Essene roots.

1846 print regarding the Last Supper[2]

---

[1] In the RCC: Anointing of the Sick (formerly known as Extreme Unction), Confirmation, Marriage, Holy Orders, Reconciliation

[2] Library of Congress - LC-DIG-pga-03395

Part One - Communion

Chapter One - Introduction to "A Brief History of Communion"

The Catholic Encyclopedia uses the following text to summarize Roman Catholic doctrine regarding the celebration of the Eucharist:

> The quintessence of these doctrinal decisions consists in this, that in the Eucharist the Body and Blood of the God-man are truly, really, and substantially present for the nourishment of our souls, by reason of the transubstantiation of the bread and wine into the Body and Blood of Christ, and that in this change of substances the unbloody Sacrifice of the New Testament is also contained. (*Catholic Encyclopedia*[3])

Contained within this doctrine are three key beliefs:

- Transubstantiation - "the body and blood of Christ are truly contained in the sacrament of the altar under the forms of bread and wine, the bread being transubstantiated into the body and the wine into the blood by divine power." (Fourth Lateran Council, 1215)
- The Real Presence of Christ during the sacrament
- The "unbloody Sacrifice" of the New Testament

All three of these doctrines have been disputed since the time of the Early Church, and like the practice of Baptism, form one of the major areas of dispute between Christian denominations. Part One of this book will trace the history of those disputes, and examine several different interpretations regarding what the celebration of the Lord's Supper is all about.

There are other areas of dispute regarding the celebration of the Lord's Supper which will be mentioned in passing in this section. These include whether the elements should be subject to "adoration", the validity of "private masses" celebrated only by a priest, and the wine versus grape juice debate.

---

[3]   http://www.newadvent.org/cathen/05572c.htm

Nomenclature

Over the millennia, several different names have been used to describe the celebration of the Lord's Supper, including:

- Eucharist (Greek: *Eucharistia*) - typically used in the Roman Catholic and Eastern Churches. It means "thanksgiving".

  G2169
  eucharistia
  yoo-khar-is-tee'-ah
  From G2170; *gratitude*; actually *grateful language* (to God, as an act of worship):—thankfulness, (giving of) thanks (-giving). (*Strong's Hebrew and Greek Dictionary*[4])

- Communion or Holy Communion (especially popular with the Reformed Church and its theological successors)
- "Agape" (Love-Feast)
- "Breaking of Bread"
- Celebration of the Lord's Supper

I've used the term "communion" in the title of this book, but any of the other terms above are perfectly valid.

Timeline

Date	Event
c. 110 A.D.	Ignatius, Bishop of Antioch is (probably) the first to use the term "Eucharist" in reference to the celebration of the Lord's Supper
c. 150 A.D.	One of the oldest depictions of the Eucharist is created in the catacomb of St. Priscilla
c. 150 A.D.	Justyn Martyr describes the rite of the Eucharist, stressing that the ceremony is for believers only
325 A.D.	Council of Nicaea forbids priests from receiving the Eucharist from deacons (18th canon)
After 604 A.D.	The term *Mass* comes into common parlance after the death of Gregory the Great, as referring to the Eucharist
1079	The term "transubstantiation" appears for the first time in a sermon by Gilbert of Savardin, Archbishop of Tours (oth-

---

[4] Parson's Technology, 1998

Date	Event
	ers say it was Hildebert of Tours around the same time period)
1202	The term "transubstantiation" appears in a papal document in a letter to the Archbishop of Lyon
1215	Transubstantiation is defined by the Fourth Lateran Council
1265-1274	Thomas Aquinas devotes 400 columns of text to the Eucharist in his *Summa Theologica*
1380s	English priest John Wycliffe writes *On the Eucharist*, which rejects transubstantiation
1414-18	Council of Constance maintains that the Mass can be proved by Scripture
1520s	Ulrich Zwingli, a Swiss Priest, writes various tracts that deny transubstantiation, the Real Presence (except in the spiritual sense), and the repetition of the sacrifice of Jesus on the Cross during the Eucharist
1536	The Lutheran Wittenberg Concord defines what will later be called the Lutheran doctrine of consubstantiation
1545-1563	Council of Trent upholds transubstantiation, Real Presence, adoration of the elements
1571	The Anglican Thirty-Nine Articles state "the Bread which we break is a partaking of the Body of Christ"; and likewise that "the Cup of Blessing is a partaking of the Blood of Christ" (Articles of Religion, Article XXVIII: Of the Lord's Supper)
1646	Westminster Confession views the sacrament symbolically and figuratively

Chapter Two - Old Testament

Reference	Notes
Genesis 14:18-20	"Then Melchizedek king of Salem brought out bread and wine. He was priest of God Most High, and he blessed Abram, saying, 'Blessed be Abram by God Most High, Creator of heaven and earth. And blessed be God Most High, who delivered your enemies into your hand.' Then Abram gave him a tenth of everything." (Genesis 14:18-20, NIV)
Exodus 12:21-28 (see also 1 Corinthians 5:6-8)	Slaughter of the Passover lamb
Proverbs 9:5	"Come, eat my food and drink the wine I have mixed."
Malachi 1:10-11	In Catholic theology, foretells the institution of a new sacrifice

Perhaps the earliest potential precursor of the celebration of the Lord's Supper in the Old Testament can be found in Genesis, in the text which describes the interactions between the mysterious Melchizedek and Abraham. Many commentators over the years have believed that Melchizedek was a pre-incarnate Christ; certainly, the New Testament book of Hebrews draws strong comparisons between Melchizedek and Christ.   Germane to our discussion here is that Melchizedek "brought out the bread and wine" and blessed Abraham, saying "Blessed be Abram by God Most High".

> Then Melchizedek king of Salem brought out bread and wine. He was priest of God Most High, and he blessed Abram, saying, "Blessed be Abram by God Most High,   Creator of heaven and earth.   And blessed be God Most High, who delivered your enemies into your hand." Then Abram gave him a tenth of everything. (Genesis 14:18-20, NIV)

Another potential precursor of the Eucharist in the Old Testament is the slaughter of the Passover lamb.

> Then Moses summoned all the elders of Israel and said to them, "Go at once and select the animals for your families and slaughter the Pas-

sover lamb. Take a bunch of hyssop, dip it into the blood in the basin and put some of the blood on the top and on both sides of the doorframe. Not one of you shall go out the door of his house until morning. When the LORD goes through the land to strike down the Egyptians, he will see the blood on the top and sides of the doorframe and will pass over that doorway, and he will not permit the destroyer to enter your houses and strike you down.

Obey these instructions as a lasting ordinance for you and your descendants. When you enter the land that the LORD will give you as he promised, observe this ceremony. And when your children ask you, "What does this ceremony mean to you?" then tell them, "It is the Passover sacrifice to the LORD, who passed over the houses of the Israelites in Egypt and spared our homes when he struck down the Egyptians." Then the people bowed down and worshiped. The Israelites did just what the LORD commanded Moses and Aaron. (Exodus 12:21-28, NIV)

c. 1874 print of Moses[5]

Paul in 1 Corinthians 5:7 explicitly links the slaughter of the Passover lamb with Christ's Last Supper.

Chapter Three - New Testament – the Last Supper

The Last Supper is described in all three Synoptic Gospels, and by Paul in 1 Corinthians. John 6 makes reference to the Lord's Supper and its meaning. Key verses include Matthew 26: 26-29, Mark 14:22-25, Luke 22: 13-20, John 6: 53-58, 1 Corinthians 10:14-17, 1 Corinthians 11:23-29.

The Last Supper[6]

So, what do the Synoptic Gospels tell us about the Last Supper? Some points of interest:

- Introduces the elements that will later be used in the Sacrament – bread and wine as the body and blood of Christ
- Gives two reasons for the Sacrament – "the blood is poured out for many – for the forgiveness of sins" and "Do this in remembrance of me"
- A new covenant replaces the old
- "I [Jesus] will not drink again of the fruit of the vine until the kingdom of God comes"

---

[6]   Library of Congress LC-USZC4-6873

While they were eating, Jesus took bread, gave thanks and broke it, and gave it to his disciples, saying, "Take and eat; this is my body."

Then he took the cup, gave thanks and offered it to them, saying, "Drink from it, all of you. This is my blood of the covenant, which is poured out for many for the forgiveness of sins. I tell you, I will not drink of this fruit of the vine from now on until that day when I drink it anew with you in my Father's kingdom." (Matthew 26: 26-29, NIV)

While they were eating, Jesus took bread, gave thanks and broke it, and gave it to his disciples, saying, "Take it; this is my body."

Then he took the cup, gave thanks and offered it to them, and they all drank from it.

"This is my blood of the covenant, which is poured out for many," he said to them. "I tell you the truth, I will not drink again of the fruit of the vine until that day when I drink it anew in the kingdom of God." (Mark 14:22-25, NIV)

They left and found things just as Jesus had told them. So they prepared the Passover.

When the hour came, Jesus and his apostles reclined at the table. And he said to them, "I have eagerly desired to eat this Passover with you before I suffer. For I tell you, I will not eat it again until it finds fulfillment in the kingdom of God."

After taking the cup, he gave thanks and said, "Take this and divide it among you. For I tell you I will not drink again of the fruit of the vine until the kingdom of God comes."

And he took bread, gave thanks and broke it, and gave it to them, saying, "This is my body given for you; do this in remembrance of me."

In the same way, after the supper he took the cup, saying, "This cup is the new covenant in my blood, which is poured out for you." (Luke 22: 13-20, NIV)

The passages in John 6 do not describe the actual Last Supper, but rather seem to describe the *importance* of the Sacrament. John uses the most graphic language out of all of the New Testament accounts, giving the impression that the bread and the wine may actually contain the body and blood of Christ.

Jesus said to them, "I tell you the truth, unless you eat the flesh of the Son of Man and drink his blood, you have no life in you. Whoever eats my flesh and drinks my blood has eternal life, and I will raise him up at the last day. For my flesh is real food and my blood is real drink. Whoever eats my flesh and drinks my blood remains in me, and I in him. Just as the living Father sent me and I live because of the Father, so the one who feeds on me will live because of me. This is the bread that came down from heaven. Your forefathers ate manna and died, but he who feeds on this bread will live forever." (John 6: 53-58, NIV)

Paul's views

In 1 Corinthians 5:6-8, Paul states "For Christ, our Passover lamb, has been sacrificed". Compare this with Exodus 12:21-28.

> Your boasting is not good. Don't you know that a little yeast works through the whole batch of dough? Get rid of the old yeast that you may be a new batch without yeast—as you really are. **For Christ, our Passover lamb, has been sacrificed**. Therefore let us keep the Festival, not with the old yeast, the yeast of malice and wickedness, but with bread without yeast, the bread of sincerity and truth. (1 Corinthians 5:6-8, NIV; emphasis added)

The account of the Last Supper that is used by most churches in their communion Sacrament comes from Paul in 1 Corinthian 11. There is some irony here, because the reason Paul provided this description was because some Christians were more focused on eating the agape meal (see next section) than on celebrating the Sacrament. Paul emphasizes the importance of eating the bread and drinking the wine in a worthy, reverent manner. He also sets the stage for later church prohibitions against open sinners taking the Sacrament.

> For I received from the Lord what I also passed on to you: The Lord Jesus, on the night he was betrayed, took bread, and when he had given thanks, he broke it and said, "This is my body, which is for you; do this in remembrance of me." In the same way, after supper he took the cup, saying, "This cup is the new covenant in my blood; do this, whenever you drink it, in remembrance of me." For whenever you eat this bread and drink this cup, you proclaim the Lord's death until he comes.

Therefore, whoever eats the bread or drinks the cup of the Lord in an unworthy manner will be guilty of sinning against the body and blood of the Lord. A man ought to examine himself before he eats of the bread and drinks of the cup. For anyone who eats and drinks without recognizing the body of the Lord eats and drinks judgment on himself. (1 Corinthians 11:23-29, NIV)

In 1 Corinthians 10, Paul notes that the Sacrament brings Christians together into a single community.

Therefore, my dear friends, flee from idolatry. I speak to sensible people; judge for yourselves what I say. Is not the cup of thanksgiving for which we give thanks a participation in the blood of Christ? And is not the bread that we break a participation in the body of Christ? Because there is one loaf, we, who are many, are one body, for we all partake of the one loaf. (1 Corinthians 10:14-17, NIV)

Chapter Four - Early Church

Various sources indicate that in the early church a fellowship meal (*agape*, the "love feast") was followed by the Eucharist ("thanksgiving"). Early Christians gave thanks during the meal and prayers were said over wine and broken bread (Acts 2:42, 2:46, 20:7, 20:11).

We discover in 1 Corinthians 11:20-29 that there were some difficulties in combining the fellowship meal with the Eucharist:

> When you come together, it is not the Lord's Supper you eat, for as you eat, each of you goes ahead without waiting for anybody else. One remains hungry, another gets drunk. Don't you have homes to eat and drink in? Or do you despise the church of God and humiliate those who have nothing? What shall I say to you? Shall I praise you for this? Certainly not! (1 Corinthians 11:20-29, NIV)

In time, the practice of combining the fellowship meal with the Eucharist faded.

The c. 96 A.D. guide for catechumens, *The Teaching of the Twelve Apostles*, gives a brief description of a Gentile church "Christian Assembly on the Lord's Day". Some points to note:

- They gathered together once a week to "break bread" (probably the agape meal)
- They gave thanksgiving (probably the Eucharist) after confession (probably public confession)
- One shouldn't partake if one is "at variance with his fellow"

> But every Lord's day do ye gather yourselves together, and break bread, and give thanksgiving after having confessed your transgressions, that your sacrifice may be pure. But let no one that is at variance with his fellow come together with you, until they be reconciled, that your sacrifice may not be profaned. For this is that which was spoken by the Lord: In every place and time offer to me a pure sacrifice; for I am a great King, saith the Lord, and my name is wonderful among the nations. (*Teaching of the Twelve Apostles*, *Fathers of the Third and Fourth Centuries*, translated by A. Cleveland Coxe, D.D.[7])

---

[7] *The Ante-Nicene Fathers Volume 7*, Edited by A. Roberts and J Donaldson

The Teaching of the Twelve Apostles also provides an ancient description of the celebration of the Eucharist. The emphasis here is on thanking God. Also, the Eucharist was reserved for baptized believers.

> Now concerning the Thanksgiving (Eucharist), thus give thanks. First, concerning the cup: We thank thee, our Father, for the holy vine of David Thy servant, which Thou madest known to us through Jesus Thy Servant; to Thee be the glory for ever. And concerning the broken bread: We thank Thee, our Father, for the life and knowledge which Thou madest known to us through Jesus Thy Servant; to Thee be the glory for ever. Even as this broken bread was scattered over the hills, and was gathered together and became one, so let Thy Church be gathered together from the ends of the earth into Thy kingdom; for Thine is the glory and the power through Jesus Christ for ever. But let no one eat or drink of your Thanksgiving (Eucharist), but they who have been baptized into the name of the Lord; for concerning this also the Lord hath said, Give not that which is holy to the dogs. (*Teaching of the Twelve Apostles*, *Fathers of the Third and Fourth Centuries*, translated by A. Cleveland Coxe, D.D.[8])

St. Ignatius of Antioch (c. 50 – c. 117)

The oldest extant use of the word *eucharist* to indicate the Lord's Supper may have been in the writings of late-first/early 2nd Century A.D. Church Father Ignatius. St. Ignatius served as the Bishop of Antioch (one source says that he was appointed as Bishop of Antioch by Peter himself.) Ignatius was friends with St. Polycarp, a successor to John the Apostle. Ignatius was martyred in Rome – according to the Catholic Encyclopedia, "he won his long-coveted crown of martyrdom in the Flavian amphitheater."

His extant writings include seven letters that he wrote to seven churches. I quote from his *Epistle to the Philadelphians* and his *Epistle to the Smyrnaeans* here. Note these points:

- Communal use of one loaf and one cup
- Administered by the bishop, or "whom he has entrusted"
- Connects the Eucharist to the agape meal

---

[8]   *Ibid*

I have confidence of you in the Lord, that ye will be of no other mind. Wherefore I write boldly to your love, which is worthy of God, and exhort you to have but one faith, and one [kind of] preaching, and one Eucharist. For there is one flesh of the Lord Jesus Christ; and His blood which was shed for us is one; one loaf also is broken to all [the communicants], and one cup is distributed among them all: there is but one altar for the whole Church, and one bishop, with the presbytery and deacons, my fellow servants. (*Epistle of Ignatius to the Philadelphians* (longer), *The Apostolic Fathers With Justin Martyr And Irenaeus*, translated by A. Cleveland Coxe, D.D.[9])

See that ye all follow the bishop, even as Jesus Christ does the Father, and the presbytery as ye would the apostles; and reverence the deacons, as being the institution of God. Let no man do anything connected with the Church without the bishop. Let that be deemed a proper Eucharist, which is [administered] either by the bishop, or by one to whom he has entrusted it. Wherever the bishop shall appear, there let the multitude [of the people] also be; even as, wherever Jesus Christ is, there is the Catholic Church. It is not lawful without the bishop either to baptize or to celebrate a love-feast; but whatsoever he shall approve of, that is also pleasing to God, so that everything that is done may be secure and valid. (The *Epistle of Ignatius to the Smyrnaeans* (shorter), *The Apostolic Fathers With Justin Martyr And Irenaeus*, translated by A. Cleveland Coxe, D.D.[10])

Justyn Martyr (c. 100 A.D. – c. 165 A.D.)

Justyn Martyr was one of the great early apologists of the Christian Church. Among his extant works are his *First Apology* and *Second Apology*. In his *First Apology* (c. 150 A.D.), Justyn Martyr gives a description of the Eucharist, again stressing that the ceremony is for believers only, and discusses the "transmutation" of the elements:

OF THE EUCHARIST

And this food is called among us Eucharistia [the Eucharist], of which no one is allowed to partake but the man who believes that the things which we teach are true, and who has been washed with the washing that is for the remission of sins, and unto regeneration, and who is so living as Christ has enjoined. For not as common bread and common drink do we receive these; but in like manner as Jesus Christ our Sa-

---

[9]   *The Ante-Nicene Fathers Volume 1*, Edited by A. Roberts and J Donaldson
[10] *Ibid*

vior, having been made flesh by the Word of God, had both flesh and blood for our salvation, so likewise have we been taught that the food which is blessed by the prayer of His word, and from which our blood and flesh by transmutation are nourished, is the flesh and blood of that Jesus who was made flesh. For the apostles, in the memoirs composed by them, which are called Gospels, have thus delivered unto us what was enjoined upon them; that Jesus took bread, and when He had given thanks, said, "This do ye in remembrance of Me, this is My body;" and that, after the same manner, having taken the cup and given thanks, He said, "This is My blood"; and gave it to them alone. Which the wicked devils have imitated in the mysteries of Mithras, commanding the same thing to be done. For, that bread and a cup of water are placed with certain incantations in the mystic rites of one who is being initiated, you either know or can learn. (*First Apology*, Justyn Martyr, c. 150 A.D., *The Apostolic Fathers With Justin Martyr And Irenaeus*, translated by A. Cleveland Coxe, D.D.[11])

Irenaeus (d. 202 A.D. ?)

Biographical information and especially dates regarding Irenaeus are sketchy at best. He was born in the first half of the 2nd century, possibly in 130 A.D., possibly in Smyrna. He knew Bishop Polycarp. He was ordained a priest and made Bishop of Lyons in the 170s A.D. He wrote his famous *Against Heresies* c. 180 A.D. He was possibly martyred in 202 A.D.

In *Against Heresies*, Irenaeus, like Ignatius, made use of the word *eucharistia*. Note also these points:

- The bread is no longer common bread after receiving the "invocation of God"
- The Eucharist gives people the hope of "resurrection to eternity"

> Then, again, how can they say that the flesh, which is nourished with the body of the Lord and with His blood, goes to corruption, and does not partake of life? Let them, therefore, either alter their opinion, or cease from offering the things just mentioned. But our opinion is in accordance with the Eucharist, and the Eucharist in turn establishes our opinion. For we offer to Him His own, announcing consistently the fellowship and union of the flesh and Spirit. For as the bread, which is produced from the earth, when it receives the invocation of God, is no longer common bread, but the Eucharist, consisting of two realit-

---

[11]   *Ibid*

ies, earthly and heavenly; so also our bodies, when they receive the Eucharist, are no longer corruptible, having the hope of the resurrection to eternity. (*Against Heresies*, Irenaeus, c. 180 A.D., *The Apostolic Fathers With Justin Martyr And Irenaeus*, translated by A. Cleveland Coxe, D.D.[12])

But vain in every respect are they who despise the entire dispensation of God, and disallow the salvation of the flesh, and treat with contempt its regeneration, maintaining that it is not capable of incorruption. But if this indeed do not attain salvation, then neither did the Lord redeem us with His blood, nor is the cup of the Eucharist the communion of His blood, nor the bread which we break the communion of His body. For blood can only come from veins and flesh, and whatsoever else makes up the substance of man, such as the Word of God was actually made. By His own blood he redeemed us, as also His apostle declares, "In whom we have redemption through His blood, even the remission of sins." And as we are His members, we are also nourished by means of the creation (and He Himself grants the creation to us, for He causes His sun to rise, and sends rain when He wills). He has acknowledged the cup (which is a part of the creation) as His own blood, from which He bedews our blood; and the bread (also a part of the creation) He has established as His own body, from which He gives increase to our bodies. (*Against Heresies*, Irenaeus, c. 180 A.D., *The Apostolic Fathers With Justin Martyr And Irenaeus*, translated by A. Cleveland Coxe, D.D.[13])

Hippolytus (died c. 236 A.D.)

Hippolytus was a presbyter of the Church of Rome in the early third century. Some sources say that he eventually became a bishop, perhaps of Rome or Porto. He was said to have been a follower of Irenaeus. Hippolytus, in his c. 215 A.D. *Apostolic Tradition* (essentially, Book 8 of the *Apostolic Constitutions*), adds these thoughts on the Eucharist:

- The Eucharist should be received before any other food
- Great care should be taken that nothing is spilled
- Sacred bread should not be left where an unbaptized person (or even a mouse) could eat it
- "And when he breaks the bread, in distributing fragments to each, he shall say: The bread of heaven in Christ Jesus."

---

[12]   *Ibid*

[13]   *Ibid*

The faithful shall be careful to partake of the eucharist before eating anything else. For if they eat with faith, even though some deadly poison is given to them, after this it will not be able to harm them.

All shall be careful so that no unbeliever tastes of the eucharist, nor a mouse or other animal, nor that any of it falls and is lost. For it is the Body of Christ, to be eaten by those who believe, and not to be scorned.

Having blessed the cup in the Name of God, you received it as the antitype of the Blood of Christ. Therefore do not spill from it, for some foreign spirit to lick it up because you despised it. You will become as one who scorns the Blood, the price with which you have been bought. (*Apostolic Tradition,* Hippolytus, c. 215 A.D.[14])

---

[14] Translation from http://www.bombaxo.com/hippolytus.html

Chapter Five - Post-Nicene Church

St. Athanasius (c. 295 A.D. – 373 A.D.)

Date	Events
c. 295	Born in Alexandria
319 A.D.	Becomes a deacon in Alexandria
c. 318 A.D,	Writes *On the Incarnation*
325 A.D.	Athanasius soundly defeats Arius at the Council of Nicaea, upholding the doctrine of the Trinity
c. 328 A.D.	Becomes Bishop (Patriarch) of Alexandria
c. 330 A.D. +	Athanasius removed (by Arian enemies) – and returned – 5 times as Bishop of Alexandria
Between 356 A.D. and 362 A.D.	Writes *The Life of St. Anthony*, about the founder of monasticism
367 A.D.	In his "thirty-ninth Letter of Holy Athanasius, Bishop of Alexandria, on the Paschal festival", Athanasius lists the books of the New Testament as we know them today
1568	Made a Doctor of the Church by Pius V

In a discourse on John 6:62-64, St. Athanasius, the defender of the doctrine of the Trinity at the Council of Nicaea, comes down strongly on the side of a spiritual, not "fleshy" interpretation. Of course, the part of John 6 traditionally viewed as specific to the Eucharist is John 6: 53-58, but his remarks could reasonably be applied to those verses, too.

> **For here also He has used both terms of Himself, flesh and spirit; and He distinguished the spirit from what is of the flesh in order that they might believe not only in what was visible in Him, but in what was invisible, and so understand that what He says is not fleshy, but spiritual. For how many would the body suffice as food, for it to become meat even for the whole world?** But this is why He mentioned the ascending of the Son of Man into heaven; namely, to draw them off from their corporeal idea, and that **from thenceforth they might understand that the aforesaid flesh was heavenly from above, and spiritual meat, to be given at His hands**. For "what I have said unto you," says He, "is spirit and life;" as much as to say, "what is manifested, and to be given for the salvation of the world, is the flesh which I

wear. But this, and the blood from it, shall be given to you spiritually at my hands as meat, so as to be imparted spiritually in each one, and to become for all a preservative to resurrection of life eternal." (*Prolegomena*, Athanasius, *St. Athanasius: Select Works And Letters*, translated by Philip Schaff, D.D., LL.D., And Henry Wace, D.D.; emphasis added[15])

St. Cyril of Jerusalem (c. 315 A.D. – 386 A.D.)

Date	Events
c. 315	Born
347	Cyril as a catechumen
By 352	Becomes a priest, and Bishop of Jerusalem
357	Cyril exiled on the charge of selling church furniture during a famine; eventually returns
359	Attends Council of Seleucia
360	Exiled a second time
361	Cyril returns to Jerusalem
367	Cyril exiled a third time
381	Attends Council of Constantinople
unknown	Canonization
1882	Designated a doctor of the Church by Pope by Leo XIII

In his work *On Sacred Liturgy and Communion*, St. Cyril of Jerusalem makes early use of the phrase "the bloodless service" in connection with the Eucharist. (Note: The Catholic Encyclopedia translates this as the "unbloody sacrifice".)

> Then, after the spiritual sacrifice, the bloodless service, is completed, over that sacrifice of propitiation we entreat God for the common peace of the Churches, for the welfare of the world; for kings; for soldiers and allies; for the sick; for the afflicted; and, in a word, for all who stand in need of succor we all pray and offer this sacrifice. (*On The Sacred Liturgy and Communion*, Lecture 23, St. Cyril of Jerusalem, translated by Philip Schaff, D.D., LL.D., And Henry Wace,D.D.[16])

---

[15] *The Nicene And Post-Nicene Fathers Second Series, Volume 4*, by Philip Schaff, editor

[16] *The Nicene And Post-Nicene Fathers, Second Series, Volume 7*, by Philip Schaff, editor

St. John Chrysostom (347 A.D. – 407 A.D.)

Date	Events
c. 347	Born in Antioch
c. 367	After meeting Bishop Meletius, begins to devote his life to the Church
381	Appointed a deacon by Bishop Meletius
c. 386	Writes *On the Priesthood*
386	Ordained as a priest by Bishop Flavian
386 - 398	Chrysostom builds reputation as the greatest preacher in Christendom
398	Ordained as Bishop (Patriarch) of Constantinople by Theophilus, Patriarch of Alexandria
401	Deposes six bishops for simony in Ephesus
403	Chrysostom is deposed based on trumped up charges made by his enemies; Chrysostom returns to Constantinople in triumph
404	Chrysostom exiled a second time
407	Dies at Commana in Pontus
438	Chrysostom's body moved to Constantinople with great pomp, and entombed in the church of the Apostles
unknown	Canonization
1568	Designated a Doctor of the Church by Pius V

St. John Chrysostom, generally considered to be the greatest preacher of his day, mentioned the Eucharist several times in his homilies. In the following commentaries on Matthew and John 6, written c. 370 A.D. and 390 A.D. (respectively), note the graphic language. We can probably assume that Chrysostom believed in both the transmutation of the elements and the Real Presence:

> Let us submit to God in all things and not contradict Him, even if what He says seems contrary to our reason and intellect; rather let His words prevail over our reason and intellect. Let us act in this way with regard to the (eucharistic) mysteries, looking not only at what falls under our senses but holding on to His words. For His word cannot lead us astray. . . When the word says, "This is My Body", be convinced of it and believe it, and look at it with the eyes of the mind. . . How many now say, "I wish I could see His shape, His appearance, His garments, His sandals." Only look! You see Him! You touch Him! You eat Him!

(*St. John Chrysostom, Homilies on the Gospel of Matthew*, St. John Chrysostom, 370 A.D.[17])

And to show the love He has for us He has made it possible for those who desire, not merely to look upon Him, but **even to touch Him and to consume Him and to fix their teeth in His Flesh and to be commingled with Him**; in short, to fulfill all their love. Let us, then, come back from that table like lions breathing out fire, thus becoming terrifying to the Devil, and remaining mindful of our Head and of the love which He has shown for us. (*St. John Chrysostom, Homily 46* (commenting on John 6), St. John Chrysostom, c. 390 A.D.; emphasis added[18])

St. Augustine (354 A.D. – 430 A.D.)

Stained glass window showing St. Augustine[19]

Date	Events
354 A.D.	Born at Tagaste
Early 1370s	Augustine as a dissolute student
Late 4th	Writes *Confessions*

[17] *The Nicene And Post-Nicene Fathers, First Series, Volume 10*, by Philip Schaff, editor

[18] *The Nicene And Post-Nicene Fathers, First Series, Volume 14*, by Philip Schaff, editor

[19] Library of Congress LAMB, no. 891 (AA size) [P&P]

Date	Events
century	
387	Baptized by St. Ambrose on Easter
391	Ordained a priest
396-430	Made Bishop of Hippo
411	Augustine soundly defeats the Donatists at the Council Of Carthage
413-426	Writes *City of God*
417-418	Augustine soundly defeats the Pelagian heresy
430	Dies in Hippo
unknown	Canonization
1295	Designated a Doctor of the Church by Boniface XIII

St. Augustine of Hippo, the greatest theologian of the early church (and the ancient theologian most quoted by Protestant reformers a 1,000 years later), provides the most well known voice in the Early Church against the idea of some sort of transmutation of the elements. In his *On Christian Doctrine*, he strongly states that the terms "eat this flesh" etc. are meant to be taken figuratively, not literally.

The *Catholic Encyclopedia* (somewhat astonishingly) brushes aside these passages by saying that Augustine must not have been freed "from the bondage of Platonism" when he wrote this. It should be underscored that Augustine's systematic theology formed the basis for Roman Catholic thought for the next 800 years, and is still influential today.

> If the sentence is one of command, either forbidding a crime or vice, or enjoining an act of prudence or benevolence, it is not figurative. If, however, it seems to enjoin a crime or vice, or to forbid an act of prudence or benevolence, it is figurative. "Except ye eat the flesh of the Son of man," says Christ, "and drink His blood, ye have no life in you." This seems to enjoin a crime or a vice; it is therefore a figure, enjoining that we should have a share in the sufferings of our Lord, and that we should retain a sweet and profitable memory of the fact that His flesh was wounded and crucified for us. Scripture says: "If thine enemy hunger, feed him; if he thirst, give him drink;" and this is beyond doubt a command to do a kindness. But in what follows, "for in so doing thou shall heap coals of fire on his head," one would think a deed of malevolence was enjoined. Do not doubt, then, that the expression is figurative; and, while it is possible to interpret it in two ways, one pointing to the doing of an injury, the other to a display of

superiority, let charity on the contrary call you back to benevolence, and interpret the coals of fire as the burning groans of penitence by which a man's pride is cured who bewails that he has been the enemy of one who came to his assistance in distress. (*On Christian Doctrine*, St. Augustine, Book 3, Chapter 16, translated by Rev. Professor J. F. Shaw[20])

---

[20] *The Nicene And Post-Nicene Fathers, First Series, Volume 2*, by Philip Schaff, editor

Chapter Six - Middle Ages

The Middle Ages were a busy time in terms of both solidifying Catholic tradition regarding the Eucharist, as well as creating an organized opposition to those traditions. It was in the Middle Ages that the term (although not necessarily the doctrine) of transubstantiation was first used.

Fourth Lateran Council

The Fourth Lateran Council of 1215 A.D., convened by Pope Innocent III, was attended by almost 1500 patriarchs, bishops, abbots and priors. Among its canons were several that had to do with the Eucharist, including these points:

- Transubstantiation was both defined and made dogma of the church
- The Eucharist must be administered by a priest
- The bread and the wine must be locked up in "properly protected places"
- Catholics must celebrate the Eucharist at least once a year

> Canon 1: There is one Universal Church of the faithful, outside of which there is absolutely no salvation. In which there is the same priest and sacrifice, Jesus Christ, whose body and blood are truly contained in the sacrament of the altar under the forms of bread and wine; the bread being changed (*transsubstantiatio*) by divine power into the body, and the wine into the blood, so that to realize the mystery of unity we may receive of Him what He has received of us. And this sacrament no one can effect except the priest who has been duly ordained in accordance with the keys of the Church, which Jesus Christ Himself gave to the Apostles and their successors.

> Canon 20: We decree that in all churches the chrism and the Eucharist be kept in properly protected places provided with locks and keys, that they may not be reached by rash and indiscreet persons and used for impious and blasphemous purposes. But if he to whom such guardianship pertains should leave them unprotected, let him be suspended from office for a period of three months. And if through his negligence an execrable deed should result, let him be punished more severely.

Canon 21: All the faithful of both sexes shall after they have reached the age of discretion faithfully confess all their sins at least once a year to their own (parish) priest and perform to the best of their ability the penance imposed, receiving reverently at least at Easter the sacrament of the Eucharist... (*Disciplinary Decrees of the General Councils: Text, Translation and Commentary*, From H. J. Schroeder[21])

The Holy Grail

St. Joseph's Chapel, Glastonbury Abbey, Somerset, England. King Arthur and Queen Guinevere were supposedly buried outside this chapel. (Photo by Robert Jones)

An interesting sidelight to any study of the history of the celebration of the Lord's Supper is to take a look at the medieval romances (in general, published in England, France and Germany between 1190 and 1520) regarding King Arthur and the search for the Holy Grail. While in some romances, the Grail takes on pagan characteristics (horn of plenty, etc.) in most of them, there is a specific Christian connection. By tradition, the Holy Grail that Arthur and his knights searched for is the Cup from the Last Supper, brought to England by Joseph of Arimithea in 63 A.D (or 37 A.D., in some accounts). Specific to our discussion here, some of the romances position achieving the Grail as a sort of alternative Mass. A good example of this genre is *The High History of the Holy Grail*, also known as *Perlesvaus* (1225). The work may have been written and published at Glastonbury Abbey, the religious site that tradition records as the spot where Joseph

---

[21]   B. Herder, 1937

brought the Grail. It is also the presumptive burial spot of Arthur and Guinevere.

In the excerpt below, King Arthur has gone to a "Chapel of St. Augustine" (probably the St. Augustine of Canterbury) in the "great forest adventurous". The Chapel was maintained by a hermit who appears to have recently died.

IArthur discovers that a Mass is being celebrated by the (assumedly dead) hermit. Arthur tries to enter, but is forced back – he is only worthy enough to observe the Mass from the doorway.

1902 print showing the Grail ceremony[22]

In some ways, the Mass is very orthodox – it describes (a very literal) transubstantiation (from the Christ child to Christ on the cross), a very literal Real Presence, and a very literal re-enactment of the sacrifice that Christ made on the cross. On the other hand, it is subtly subversive, as the "elements" (in this case, the Christ child) are not offered up by the priest, but by Mary; and the Mass is not conducted by a priest, but rather the hermit who had only become a Christian five years before.

---

[22] Library of Congress LC-USZ62-133683

The King goeth to the bar whereby one entereth into the launde, and looketh to the right into a combe of the forest and seeth the chapel of S. Augustine and the right fair hermitage. Thitherward goeth he and alighteth, and it seemeth him that the hermit is apparelled to sing the mass. He reineth up his horse to the bough of a tree by the side of the chapel and thinketh to enter hereinto, but, had it been to conquer all the kingdoms of the world, thereinto might he not enter, albeit there was none made him denial thereof, for the door was open and none saw he that might forbid him. Sore ashamed is the King thereof. Howbeit, he beholdeth an image of Our Lord that was there within and crieth Him of mercy right sweetly, and looketh toward the altar. And he looketh at the holy hermit that was robed to sing mass and said his Confiteor [prayer], he seeth at his right hand the fairest Child that ever he had seen, and He was clad in an alb [a linen vestment with narrow sleeves] and had a golden crown on his head loaded with precious stones that gave out a full great brightness of light. On the left hand side, was a Lady so fair that all the beauties of the world might not compare them with her beauty. When the holy hermit had said his Confiteor and went to the altar, the Lady also took her Son and went to sit on the right hand side towards the altar upon a right rich chair and set her Son upon her knees and began to kiss Him full sweetly and saith: 'Sir,' saith she, "You are my Father and my Son and my Lord, and guardian of me and of all the world."

King Arthur heareth the words and seeth the beauty of the Lady and of the Child, and marvelleth much of this that She should call Him her Father and her Son. He looketh at a window behind the altar and seeth a flame come through at the very instant that mass was begun, clearer than any ray of sun nor moon nor star, and evermore it threw forth a brightness of light such that and all the lights in the world had been together it would not have been the like. And it is come down upon the altar. King Arthur seeth it who marvelleth him much thereof. But sore it irketh him of this that he may not enter therewithin, and he heareth, there where the holy hermit was singing the mass, right fair responses, and they seem him to be the responses of angels. And when the Holy Gospel was read, King Arthur looked toward the altar and saw that the Lady took her Child and offered Him into the hands of the holy hermit, but of this King Arthur made much marvel, that the holy hermit washed not his hands when he had received the offering. Right sore did King Arthur marvel him thereof, but little right would he have had to marvel had he known the reason. And when the Child was offered him, he set Him upon the altar and thereafter began his sacrament. And King Arthur set him on his knees before the chapel and began to pray to God and to beat his breast. And he looked toward the altar after the preface, and it seemed him that the holy hermit held between his hands a man bleeding from His side and in His palms and in His feet, and crowned with thorns, and he seeth Him in His own figure. And when he had looked on Him so long and knoweth not what is become of Him, the King hath pity of Him in his heart of this that he had seen, and the tears of his heart come into his eyes. And he looketh toward the altar and thinketh to see the figure of the man, and seeth that it is changed into the shape of the Child that he had seen tofore. (*The High History of the Holy Grail*, translation by Sebastian Evans, 1898; reprinted in *An Arthurian Reader*, edited by John Matthews[23])

---

[23] The Aquarian Press, 1988

Chapter Seven – Reformation

c. 1874 print "Heroes of the Reformation"[24]

John Wycliffe (c. 1330 - 1384)

Date	Event
c. 1330	Wycliffe born in Yorkshire, England
1361	Ordained priest (See of Lincoln)
1372	Doctorate of Theology
1374/76	Publishes *Tractatus de civili dominio*
1377	Brought to trial before Archbishop of Canterbury as a heretic; saved by the crowds
1377	Pope condemns 18 propositions of Wycliffe (in 5 separate bulls)
1380s	Writes *On the Eucharist*
1381/84	Begins first full English translation of the Bible (from Jerome's Latin Vulgate). Published in 1388.
1415	Condemned by Council of Constance for 267 heresies
1428	Remains dug up and burned on papal order

In the 1380s, a prominent English priest named John Wycliffe spoke out against the doctrine of transubstantiation. (However, Wycliffe

---

[24] Library of Congress LC-DIG-pga-02660

believed in the "Real Presence" of Christ during the Eucharist - "spiritually, truly, really, effectively".)   In his work *On the Eucharist*, he stated:

> But the simplest layman will see that it follows, that inasmuch as this bread is the body of Christ, it is therefore bread, and remains bread, and is at once both bread and the body of Christ.

> In the same manner, accordingly, though the bread becometh the body of Christ, by virtue of his words, it need not cease to be bread.

> We are thus shut up, either to destroy the verity of Scripture, or to go along with the senses and the judgment of mankind, and admit that it is bread. Mice, and other creatures, are aware of this fact; for according to philosophers, they have the power of discerning what is good for them to eat. Oh, if believer's in the Lord will look on, and see Antichrist and his accomplices so strong as to have power to condemn and persecute even unto death, those sons of the church who thus yield their belief to the Gospel, yet certain I am, that though the truth of the Gospel may for a time be cast down in the streets, and be kept under in a measure by the threats of Antichrist, yet extinguished it cannot be, since he who is the Truth has said, that "'heaven and earth shall pass away, but that his words shall not pass away!" Let the believer, then, rouse himself, and demand strictly from our heretics, what the nature of this venerable sacrament is, if it be not bread; since the language of the Gospel, the evidence of our senses, and arguments that have in their favour every probability, say that so it is.

> Beyond all doubt, then, the expression "this is my body," is figurative, as are those in the Gospel of John: "unless ye eat the flesh of the Son of Man", with many like them, which Christ spake in another sense. (*Tracts and Treatises John De Wycliffe D.D.*, Blackburn and Pardon, 1845[25])

---

[25]   Reprinted by Google Books

Martin Luther (1483 – 1546)

1882 print of Martin Luther[26]

Date	Events
1483	Born in Eisleben, Saxony
1505/07	Becomes Augustinian monk; ordained as a priest
1512	Doctorate in Theology; Professor of Biblical Literature at Wittenburg University
1517	Protests sale of indulgences by Pope Leo X
October 31, 1517	Tacks 95 theses to door of Wittenburg Castle
1521	Luther excommunicated
April 17/18, 1521	Council (Diet) of Worm, convened by Charles V, Emperor of the Holy Roman Empire. Luther ordered to recant. Luther replies, "Here I stand. I can do no other."
1521-1522	Luther in hiding at Wartburg Castle; translates New Testament into German, and battles with the Devil
1527	Writes "A Mighty Fortress is Our God" (Luther wrote a

[26] Library of Congress LC-DIG-pga-02205

Date	Events
	total of 41 hymns)
1528	Publishes "Large Catechism", "Small Catechism"
1530	Luther is the doctrinal inspiration for the Augsburg Confession
1534	Publishes German Bible - 100,000 copies of New Testament printed in Wittenberg during his lifetime

As Wycliffe had 150 years earlier, Martin Luther would come to the conclusion that, while there may not be a chemical change in the elements during the Eucharist, "the true body and blood of our Lord Jesus Christ, [is] in and under the bread and wine". This view was later called, by some, consubstantiation. Luther also strongly believed in the Real Presence.

In his *The Large Catechism*, Luther answered the question "Now, what is the Sacrament of the Altar?" with:

> It is the true body and blood of our Lord Jesus Christ, in and under the bread and wine which we Christians are commanded by the Word of Christ to eat and to drink. And as we have said of Baptism that it is not simple water, so here also we say the Sacrament is bread and wine, but not mere bread and wine, such as are ordinarily served at the table, but bread and wine comprehended in, and connected with, the Word of God.
>
> It is the Word (I say) which makes and distinguishes this Sacrament, so that it is not mere bread and wine, but is, and is called, the body and blood of Christ...
>
> With this Word you can strengthen your conscience and say: If a hundred thousand devils, together with all fanatics, should rush forward, crying, How can bread and wine be the body and blood of Christ? etc., I know that all spirits and scholars together are not as wise as is the Divine Majesty in His little finger. Now here stands the Word of Christ: Take, eat; this is My body; Drink ye all of it; this is the new testament in My blood, etc. Here we abide, and would like to see those who will constitute themselves His masters, and make it different from what He has spoken. It is true, indeed, that if you take away the Word or regard it without the words, you have nothing but mere bread and wine. But if the words remain with them as they shall and must, then, in virtue of the same, it is truly the body and blood of Christ. For as the lips of Christ say and speak, so it is, as He can never lie or deceive.

(*The Large Catechism*, Martin Luther, translated by F. Bente and W.H.T. Dau, Published in *Triglot Concordia: The Symbolical Books of the Ev. Lutheran Church*[27])

In 1530, Luther's views on the Eucharist were officially incorporated as a tenet of Lutheranism in the Augsburg Confession:

Of the Lord's Supper: "..the [true] body and blood of Christ are truly present [under the form of bread and wine], and are [there] communicated to those that eat in the Lord's supper..." (*The Augsburg Confession*, by Philip Melanchthon[28])

Luther's belief in the Real Presence caused a split in the ranks of his own followers, as this 1525 letter from Luther indicates:

Carlstadt, who is quite given over to the devil, rages against me, having issued various writings full of poison. He, with his followers, denies that the body and blood of Christ are present in the Sacrament. I am ready to confute him, although through artifice, as he has led many astray in different places. (*Letter 113, To John Brismann, Konigsberg*, Martin Luther, January 11, 1525, *The Letters of Martin Luther*[29])

Ulrich Zwingli (1484 - 1531)

Date	Events
1484	Born in Wildhaus, Switzerland
1506	Master of Arts, University of Basel; becomes a priest - Influenced by writings of Erasmus
1518	Appointed preacher at Grossmunster Cathedral in Zurich - Leads Zurich to withdrawal from alliance with Catholic France
1522	Resigns from priesthood; employed by Zurich City Council as evangelical pastor
1523	Publishes *67 Theses*
1525/1526	Authorizes execution of the Anabaptists
1531	Dies fighting in Catholic/Protestant Second War of Kappel

Ulrich Zwingli, often considered the founder of the Reformed Church tradition, would take things a step further than Luther and Wycliffe, and deny transubstantiation, the Real Presence, (at least in the way it

---

[27] Concordia Publishing House, 1921
[28] Ages Software, 1997
[29] Ages Software, 1997

had traditionally been understood), and the repetition of the Sacrifice of Jesus on the cross. Zwingli (like Augustine a 1,000 years before) believed that the "this bread is my body" etc. verbiage in the New Testament was meant to be taken symbolically. He believed in a "spiritual eating", efficacious through faith in Jesus Christ, not through the words of the Sacrament. In his work *On Predestination, Baptism, and the Eucharist*, Zwingli wrote:

> I believe that in the holy Eucharist, i.e., the supper of thanksgiving, the true body of Christ is present by the contemplation of faith. This means that they who thank the Lord for the benefits bestowed on us in His Son acknowledge that He assumed true flesh, in it truly suffered, truly washed away our sins by His blood; and thus everything done by Christ becomes as it were present to them by the contemplation of faith. But that the body of Christ in essence and really, i. e., the natural body itself, is either present in the supper or masticated with our mouth and teeth, as the Papists or some [i.e., the Lutherans] who look back to the fleshpots of Egypt assert, we not only deny, but constantly maintain to be an error, contrary to the Word of God.

> In view of these passages we are compelled to confess that the words: "This is my body," should not be understood naturally, but fig-uratively, just as the words: "This is Jehovah's passover" [Ex. 12: 11]...

> Let them who wish go now and condemn us for heresy, only let them know that by the same process they are condemning the opinions of the theologians, contrary to the decrees of the Pontiffs. For from these facts it becomes very evident that the ancients [Ambrose and Augustine] always spoke figuratively when they attributed so much to the eating of the body of Christ in the Supper; meaning, not that sac-ramental eating could cleanse the soul but faith in God through Jesus Christ, which is spiritual eating, whereof this external eating is but symbol and shadow. And as bread sustains the body and wine en-livens and exhilarates, thus it strengthens the soul and assures it of God's mercy that He has given us His Son; thus it renews the mind by the confidence that, by His blood, the sins with which it was being consumed were destroyed... (*On Predestination, Baptism, and the Eucharist*, Ulrich Zwingli, *Ulrich Zwingli, An Account of the Faith of Huldereich Zwingli Submitted to the Roman Emperor Charles (3 July 1530)*, translated by S. M. Macauley, *The Latin Works and Corres-pondence of Huldreich Zwingli, vol. 2*[30])

---

[30]   Heidelberg Press, 1922

John Calvin (1509 - 1564)

Date	Events
1509	Born in Noyon, France
1523	Studies for priesthood in Paris
1528/29	Studies law in Orleans, Bourges
1533	"Conversion" - Breaks with Roman Church
1536	• Publishes *Institutes of the Christian Religion* • Flees to Geneva Switzerland, which declared for the Reformed Faith two months before Calvin arrived • At the urging of William Farel, becomes an evangelical preacher in Geneva
April 23, 1538	Farel and Calvin deposed by the Great Council of Geneva – Calvin goes to Strasbourg, Farel to Basel
1541	Prodded by commercial interests, and fear of a revived Catholicism, the Great Council asked Farel and Calvin to return to Geneva
1541/1564	Theocratic ruler of the "City of God" in Geneva, Switzerland
1542	"Ecclesiastical Ordinances" passed - Government of the Reformed Church established (no bishops, cardinals, etc.)
1610	Long after Calvin's death, Dutch Calvinist's debate Arminians (believers in free will) in Dort; the Calvinist's develop the acronym TULIP[31] to describe Calvin's theology.

John Calvin, essentially the successor to Ulrich Zwingli in the Reformed Church, took similar views on the Communion. He believed that there was no sacrifice involved – the Sacrament is a memorial. Further, he thought that the "eat this body" language should be taken figuratively, and that if Christ is present during the Sacrament, it is through the Spirit.

To represent Calvin's views, I've quoted from his *Commentary on 1 Corinthians* below.

> Nothing is more manifest than that their Mass is diametrically opposed to the sacred Supper of our Lord. I go farther — we show in the plainest manner, that it is full of wicked abominations: hence there is need of reformation...

---

[31] Total Depravity, Unconditional Election, Limited Atonement, Irresistible Grace, Perseverance of the Saints

...For the meaning of the words is: "By participating in the breaking of bread, according to the order and observance which I have prescribed, you shall be participants also in my body." Hence, when an individual eats of it by himself, the promise in that case goes for nothing. Besides, we are taught in these words what the Lord would have us do. Take, says he. Hence those that offer a sacrifice to God have some other than Christ as their authority, for we are not instructed in these words to perform a sacrifice.

Let us regard it then as beyond all controversy that Christ is here speaking of the bread. Now the question is — "In what sense?" That we may elicit the true meaning, we must hold that the expression is figurative; for, assuredly, to deny this is exceedingly dishonest. Why then is the term body applied to the bread? All, I think, will allow that it is for the same reason that John calls the Holy Spirit a dove. John 1:32.) Thus far we are agreed. Now the reason why the Spirit was so called was this — that he had appeared in the form of a dove. Hence the name of the Spirit is transferred to the visible sign. Why should we not maintain that there is here a similar instance of metonymy [symbolism], and that the term body is applied to the bread, as being the sign and symbol of it?

...The statue of Hercules is called Hercules, but what have we there but a bare, empty representation? On the other hand the Spirit is called a dove, as being a sure pledge of the invisible presence of the Spirit. Hence the bread is Christ's body, because it assuredly testifies, that the body which it represents is held forth to us, or because the Lord, by holding out to us that symbol, gives us at the same time his own body; for Christ is not a deceiver, to mock us with empty representations. Hence it is regarded by me as beyond all controversy, that the reality is here conjoined with the sign; or, in other words, that we do not less truly become participants in Christ's body in respect of spiritual efficacy, than we partake of the bread.

...I conclude, that Christ's body is really, (as the common expression is,) — that is, truly given to us in the Supper, to be wholesome food for our souls. I use the common form of expression, but my meaning is, that our souls are nourished by the substance of the body, that we may truly be made one with him, or, what amounts to the same thing, that **a life-giving virtue from Christ's flesh is poured into us by the Spirit, though it is at a great distance from us, and is not mixed with us**.

...But that participation in the body of Christ, which, I affirm, is presented to us in the Supper, does not require a local presence, nor

the descent of Christ, nor infinite extension, nor anything of that nature, for the Supper being a heavenly action, there is no absurdity in saying, that Christ, while remaining in heaven, is received by us. **For as to his communicating himself to us, that is effected through the secret virtue of his Holy Spirit**, which can not merely bring together, but join in one, things that are separated by distance of place, and far remote.

But, in order that we may be capable of this participation, we must rise heavenward. Here, therefore, faith must be our resource, when all the bodily senses have failed.

Do this in remembrance of me. **Hence the Supper is a memorial**, appointed as a help to our weakness; for if we were sufficiently mindful of the death of Christ, this help would be unnecessary. (*Commentary On The First Epistle To The Corinthians,* John Calvin, translated by the Rev. John Pringle; emphasis added[32])

Caspar Schwenckfeld (1489-1561)

Date	Events
1489	Born in Ossig, Silesia, Germany
1518	"Visitation of the divine" - Schwenckfeld's conversion - becomes early follower of Luther
1524	Writes *Admonition*
1525	Schwenckfeld-Luther debate
1541	Writes "Great Confession"
1547-1563	Entire body of Schwenckfeld's works banned by the Council of Trent - an honor shared with Luther and Calvin
1561	Death of Schwenckfeld
1734	Schwenkfelders flee from Jesuit persecution to Pennsylvania
1826	Last Schwenkfelder in Europe dies

Schwenckfeld, although an early follower of Luther, ended up disagreeing with Luther on the subject of communion. Schwenckfeld took what is now sometimes viewed as the "spiritual" interpretation of the Eucharist. He felt that, just as the bread and wine can provide physical nourishment to the body, they also provide spiritual nourishment:

---

[32] Ages Software, 1997

It was not until the disciples had eaten the bread and drunk the wine that Christ spoke the words. Bread is not a food until the grain has been grown, threshed, ground, baked and eaten; bread when eaten nourishes and strengthens the body.

Give the physical to the body, spiritual to the poor soul which is spiritual; let physical bread nourish the physical body, the invisible [bread], the invisible soul. (*Casper Schwenckfeld: Forgotten Reformer*[33])

Also, Schwenckfeld believed that Christians should not take communion when in open discord (see 1 Corinthians 11:27). Schwenckfeld halted communion among his followers because of this view, and the ban lasted for several centuries!!

Westminster Confession and Catechism

The Westminster Confession (1646) and the Westminster Larger Catechism (1648) have a series of statements (the former) and questions and answers (the latter) that discuss the nature of the Lord's Supper (Communion). The catechism and confession were largely the work of 17th century English and Scottish Calvinists, and codified the views of Calvin and Zwingli. Key precepts:

- Denies transubstantiation
- Christ is present only in a spiritual sense
- Communicants must properly prepare themselves before taking communion
- There is no sacrifice, only a commemoration

Westminster Confession

29:2 In this sacrament, Christ is not offered up to His Father; nor any real sacrifice made at all for remission of sins of the quick or the dead (Heb 9:22, 25, 26, 28); but only a commemoration of that one offering up of Himself, by Himself, upon the cross, once for all: and a spiritual oblation of all possible praise unto God for the same (Matt 26:26, 27; 1 Cor 11:24-26): so that the Popish sacrifice of the mass (as they call it) is most abominably injurious to Christ's one, only sacrifice, the alone propitiation for all the sins of His elect (Heb 7:23, 24, 27; 10:11, 12, 14, 18).

---

[33] *Christian History*, Issue 21, January 1989

29:4 Private masses, or receiving this sacrament by a priest or any other alone (1 Cor 10:6); as likewise, the denial of the cup to the people (Mark 4:23; 1 Cor 11:25-29), worshipping the elements, the lifting them up or carrying them about for adoration, and the reserving them for any pretended religious use; are all contrary to the nature of this sacrament, and to the institution of Christ (Matt 15:9).

29:6 That doctrine which maintains a change of the substance of bread and wine, into the substance of Christ's body and blood (commonly called transubstantiation) by consecration of a priest, or by any other way, is repugnant, not to Scripture alone, but even to common sense and reason; overthroweth the nature of the sacrament, and hath been, and is the cause of manifold superstitions; yea, of gross idolatries (Luke 24:6, 39; Acts 3:21 with 1 Cor 11:24-26).

Westminster Larger Catechism

Question 170: How do they that worthily communicate in the Lord's Supper feed upon the body and blood of Christ therein?

Answer: As the body and blood of Christ are not corporally or carnally present in, with, or under the bread and wine in the Lord's Supper, and yet are spiritually present to the faith of the receiver, no less truly and really than the elements themselves are to their outward senses; so they that worthily communicate in the sacrament of the Lord's Supper, do therein feed upon the body and blood of Christ, not after a corporal and carnal, but in a spiritual manner; yet truly and really, while by faith they receive and apply unto themselves Christ crucified, and all the benefits of his death.

Question 171: How are they that receive the sacrament of the Lord's Supper to prepare themselves before they come unto it?

Answer: They that receive the sacrament of the Lord's Supper are, before they come, to prepare themselves thereunto, by examining themselves of their being in Christ, of their sins and wants; of the truth and measure of their knowledge, faith, repentance; love to God and the brethren, charity to all men, forgiving those that have done them wrong; of their desires after Christ, and of their new obedience; and by renewing the exercise of these graces, by serious meditation, and fervent prayer.

Question 173: May any who profess the faith, and desire to come to the Lord's Supper, be kept from it?

Answer: Such as are found to be ignorant or scandalous, notwithstanding their profession of the faith, and desire to come to the Lord's Supper, may and ought to be kept from that sacrament, by the power which Christ has left in his church, until they receive instruction, and manifest their reformation.

Question 174: What is required of them that receive the sacrament of the Lord's Supper in the time of the administration of it?

Answer: It is required of them that receive the sacrament of the Lord's Supper, that, during the time of the administration of it, with all holy reverence and attention they wait upon God in that ordinance, diligently observe the sacramental elements and actions, heedfully discern the Lord's body, and affectionately meditate on his death and sufferings, and thereby stir up themselves to a vigorous exercise of their graces; in judging themselves, and sorrowing for sin; in earnest hungering and thirsting after Christ, feeding on him by faith, receiving of his fullness, trusting in his merits, rejoicing in his love, giving thanks for his grace; in renewing of their covenant with God, and love to all the saints.

Chapter Eight - Council of Trent

By the 1540s, the Roman Catholic Church was reeling from the affects of Protestantism all through Europe. While once the pope reigned supreme over all of Western Christendom, by 1540, whole countries had been lost to Protestant usurpers, including England (Henry VIII), Germany (Luther) and Switzerland (Calvin). France, too, was starting to look shaky, as a growing community of Calvinists were asserting their rights there. And (unthinkably!) Protestantism was even making inroads into Italy itself! The Roman Church viewed that something must be done to stem the tide of defections. The set of methodologies employed to do so is collectively known as the Counter-Reformation.

The Counter-Reformation used several methods to attempt to save the church. Among these were the creation of a new militant religious order (the Jesuits), open warfare against Protestant strongholds (The 30 Years War in Germany), and reconstituting the Inquisition. Germane to this discussion is one more method used - to call a great church council. The Council of Trent met from 1545–1563, and enacted many church reforms, and restated basic Catholic beliefs. Among the canons on the Eucharist:

> CANON I.-If any one denieth, that, in the sacrament of the most holy Eucharist, are contained truly, really, and substantially, the body and blood together with the soul and divinity of our Lord Jesus Christ, and consequently the whole Christ; but saith that He is only therein as in a sign, or in figure, or virtue; let him be anathema.

> CANON II.-If any one saith, that, in the sacred and holy sacrament of the Eucharist, the substance of the bread and wine remains conjointly with the body and blood of our Lord Jesus Christ, and denieth that wonderful and singular conversion of the whole substance of the bread into the Body, and of the whole substance of the wine into the Blood-the species Only of the bread and wine remaining-which conversion indeed the Catholic Church most aptly calls Transubstantiation; let him be anathema.

> CANON III.-If any one denieth, that, in the venerable sacrament of the Eucharist, the whole Christ is contained under each species, and un-

der every part of each species, when separated; let him be anathema…

CANON VI.-If any one saith, that, in the holy sacrament of the Euchar-ist, Christ, the only-begotten Son of God, is not to be adored with the worship, even external of latria [adoration, supreme honor]; and is, consequently, neither to be venerated with a special festive solem-nity, nor to be solemnly borne about in processions, according to the laudable and universal rite and custom of holy church; or, is not to be proposed publicly to the people to be adored, and that the adorers thereof are idolators; let him be anathema…

CANON VIII.-If any one saith, that Christ, given in the Eucharist, is eaten spiritually only, and not also sacramentally and really; let him be anathema…

CANON XI.-If any one saith, that faith alone is a sufficient preparation for receiving the sacrament of the most holy Eucharist; let him be anathema. And for fear lest so great a sacrament may be received un-worthily, and so unto death and condemnation, this holy Synod or-dains and declares, that sacramental confession, when a confessor may be had, is of necessity to be made beforehand, by those whose conscience is burthened with mortal sin, how contrite even soever they may think themselves. But if any one shall presume to teach, preach, or obstinately to assert, or even in public disputation to de-fend the contrary, he shall be thereupon excommunicated. (*The Council of Trent, The Thirteenth Session, The canons and decrees of the sacred and ecumenical Council of Trent*, Edited and translated by J. Waterworth[34])

---

[34] Dolman, 1848

Chapter Nine - Catholic practice

1848 print showing aspects of the Eucharist[35]

In the early 2000s, I had a young married couple attending my Sunday School class. The wife was a life-long Protestant; the husband was a life-long Roman Catholic. On her first visit to her husband's home church, she was in line to receive the Eucharist. Somehow it was indicated to her that, since she wasn't a practicing Catholic, she couldn't partake of the Eucharist. She started to walk away, with the communion wafer in her hands. According to her, "the priest ran after me, and practically tackled me to get the wafer back. I was so embarrassed – I'll never go to a Catholic Church again."

As a life-long Evangelical Protestant, I can't picture such an incident happening in, say, a Presbyterian church, the U.C.C., or a Baptist

35   Library of Congress LC-USZC2-2581

church. So, why did it happen in a Catholic church? If you believe in the three things that we identified at the beginning of this section as key Catholic beliefs on the Eucharist, it becomes clearer:

- Transubstantiation - "the body and blood of Christ are truly contained in the sacrament of the altar under the forms of bread and wine, the bread being transubstantiated into the body and the wine into the blood by divine power." (Fourth Lateran Council, 1215)
- The Real Presence of Christ during the sacrament
- The "unbloody Sacrifice" of the New Testament

If you really believe the physical body and blood of Jesus Christ is present during the Sacrament, and you believe that you are performing the "unbloody Sacrifice" of the New Testament, than the actual elements (and how they are treated) become a key area of focus. There are other Catholic practices that come out of the above three beliefs:

- "According to the law of today (Council of Trent, Sess. XXII, de reform.), the Mass may be celebrated only in Chapels and public (or semi-public) oratories, which must be consecrated or at least blessed." (*Catholic Encyclopedia*[36])
- "The altar-cross is also necessary as an indication that the Sacrifice of the Mass is nothing else than the unbloody reproduction of the Sacrifice of the Cross." (*Catholic Encyclopedia*[37])
- The requirement that each church have a tabernacle, "the name for the receptacle or case placed upon the table of the high altar or of another altar in which the vessels containing the Blessed Sacrament...are kept (*Catholic Encyclopedia*[38])".

According to the Sacred Congregation of Rites, "this tabernacle must be safe and inviolable". Some Medieval Synods added a requirement that the tabernacle have a lock.

---

[36] http://www.newadvent.org/cathen/10006a.htm
[37] *Ibid*
[38] http://www.newadvent.org/cathen/14424a.htm

"Girl at first communion c. 1900"[39]

Chapter Ten - And Protestants today...

Dr. Bryant Harris, Senior Pastor of Mars Hill Presbyterian Church in Acworth, GA, prepares to celebrate communion in 2007

If we look at modern Protestantism, the celebration of the Lord's Supper can be viewed as a continuum, with those Protestant denominations closest to Catholic practice (Anglican, Lutheran) on one side of the continuum, and those that take a commemorative/figurative or spiritual view on the other end of the continuum (Presbyterian, U.C.C., Baptist, Church of the Nazarene, etc.) The Methodist Church is somewhere in the middle, rejecting transubstantiation, but believing in the Real Presence.

It is probably worth noting that there is some degree of ambivalence in the Anglican view of celebrating the Lord's Supper. While the Anglican Thirty-Nine Articles state "the Bread which we break is a partaking of the Body of Christ"; and likewise that "the Cup of Blessing is a partaking of the Blood of Christ", other Anglican documents view "Communion as a spiritual mystery".

It should be noted that almost all Protestant denominations reject the adoration of the elements.

As noted previously, Roman Catholics only allow practicing Catholics to receive the Eucharist. Some Protestant Churches also practice "closed" communion, including the Missouri Synod of the Lutheran Church, and some Mennonite groups. Most Protestant denominations practice "open" communion, although some require that the participants be baptized Christians (as was seen in the chapter of this section on the Early Church, this practice dates from a very early time). In the Presbyterian Church communion is typically open to "anyone that accepts Jesus Christ as their Savior".

Wine vs. grape juice

One of the arguments within Protestantism is whether wine or grape juice should be used to represent the "blood of Christ". Those on the wine side of the issue nod towards church tradition, and note that Jesus and the Apostles would have used the drink common in the Passover ceremony which was wine. Those on the grape juice side often have Calvinist roots, and abhor all use of (drinkable) alcohol for any reason.

Here is the Greek word used in the Bible:

> G129
> aima
> hah'ee-mah
> Of uncertain derivation; *blood*, literally (of men or animals), figuratively (**the *juice* of grapes**) or specifically (the atoning *blood* of Christ); by implication *bloodshed*, also *kindred:*—blood. (*Strong's Hebrew and Greek Dictionaries;* emphasis added[40])

Going strictly by the definition above, it would seem that either wine or grape juice would be acceptable for the Sacrament.

---

[40]   Parson's Technology, 1998

Part Two - Baptism

Chapter Eleven - Introduction to "A Brief History of Baptism"

> BAPTISM is the initiatory sign by which we are admitted to the fellowship of the Church, that being engrafted into Christ we may be accounted children of God. Moreover, the end for which God has given it (this I Have shown to be common to all mysteries) is, first, that it may be conducive to our faith in him; and, secondly, that it may serve the purpose of a confession among men. (*Institutes of the Christian Religion*, John Calvin, translated by Henry Beveridge[41])
>
> Baptism is a manifestation of the Father's prevenient love, a sharing in the Son's Paschal Mystery, and a communication of new life in the Spirit; it brings people into the inheritance of God and joins them to the Body of Christ, the Church. (*Instruction On Infant Baptism*, By the Sacred Congregation for the Doctrine of the Faith; Approved by His Holiness Pope John Paul II, October 20, 1980)

The term "baptism" comes from the Greek word *baptizo,* which means to "immerse, dip, submerge". Few Christians would argue the importance of Baptism - yet few topics have caused such controversy in the history of the Universal Church. Debates such as the following continue even today:

- Is baptism necessary to salvation?
- Is infant baptism supported by the Scriptures, or should only "believers" be baptized?
- If part of the reason for baptism is the remission of sins, what about sins committed after baptism?
- How should the baptism ceremony be conducted - should catechumens be immersed, or only "sprinkled"?
- What happens if someone is baptized by a priest or minister who is later excommunicated or who breaks away from the church? Is the baptism still "good"?
- Should people be "rebaptized" if they leave one denomination for another?

---

[41] AGES Software, 1996

How different Christian groups respond to these and other questions can lead to situations such as schisms (the Donatists and Pelagians with the Catholic Church) and persecution (the Anabaptists in the early days of the Protestant Reformation).

Part Two of this book will give a brief history of Christian Baptism, using the historical panoply to introduce some of the theological arguments for and against various baptism practices and beliefs. Topics will include baptism in the Bible, baptism in the early church, the Donatist/Pelagian controversies of the 4th and 5th centuries (and the huge impact that St. Augustine of Hippo had on the views of the Catholic Church on baptism), and the Protestant battles regarding infant baptism that were to come a thousand years later.

Baptism Timeline

Date	Event
c. 182/88 A.D.	Irenaeus in "Against Heresies" may be the first to specifically mention infant baptism
c. 215	Hippolytus in the "Apostolic Tradition" states "First Baptize the children"
c. 250	Some Christians commit apostasy under the persecution of Decian
c. 251	Novatian, a presbyter of Rome, breaks away from the Catholic Church after apostate priests are readmitted to the Church
c. 254-256	Cyprian of Carthage argues that baptisms given by schismatics are invalid; Bishop Stephen of Rome holds that the sacraments belong not to the minister but to Christ
303–306	Diocletian's persecution of Christians
311 & 315	First Majorinus, and then Donatus set up as rival bishops of Carthage, after a bishop is ordained by a possible apostate. "Donatists" believed a) only Donatist baptisms are valid and b) baptisms performed by the unworthy are invalid.
c. 312	Conversion of Constantine to Christianity
314	Donatism condemned by the Council of Arles
337	Constantine is baptized shortly before his death
c. 380	British monk Pelagius is shocked by lax morals among Christians in Rome. He eventually rejects the doctrines of Grace and Original Sin, but still believes that infants should be baptized (John 3:5).
387	St. Augustine baptized by St. Ambrose

Date	Event
393	Augustine begins his offensive against the Donatists
411	Arbitration in Carthage rules in favor of Augustine, and against the Donatists
412 – 421	Augustine writes thirteen works and letters denouncing the views of Pelagius – Augustine believes that we are all tainted by original sin; unbaptized children are condemned to "darkness"
418	Council of Carthage condemns "whoever says that new-born infants should not be baptized"
418	Pelagius excommunicated by Pope Zosimus
431	Pelagian heresy condemned at the Council of Ephesus
1412	Council of Florence states that infants should receive baptism "as soon as is convenient"
January 21, 1525	Several students of Ulrich Zwingli illegally rebaptize themselves in Zurich, starting the Anabaptist movement
1536	John Calvin publishes "Christian Institutes"
1528	Luther states in his Large Catechism "we must be baptized or we cannot be saved"
1609	Englishman John Smyth re-baptizes 40 followers in Amsterdam, starting the Baptist movement
1644	Baptist congregations in London draw up First London Confession, with believers' baptism by immersion as a central tenet
1649	Westminster Confession affirms infant baptism, but views that baptism is not necessary for salvation
c. 1906	Birth of Pentecostalism, with its emphasis on "baptism with the Holy Ghost and fire"
1980	Pope John Paul II strongly reaffirms the necessity for infant baptism, in the "Instruction On Infant Baptism" by the Sacred Congregation for the Doctrine of the Faith

Chapter Twelve - Baptism in the Old Testament

There is no explicit reference in the Old Testament to baptism, although some commentaries point out that baptism was practiced during the end of the inter-testamental period by Jews initiating Gentile converts into Judaism.

While there is no explicit reference to baptism in the Old Testament as we understand it in the Christian sense, there are references to various elements that would eventually assert themselves in Christian baptism, such as the use of water for ceremonial purification, the pouring out of the Holy Spirit on individuals, and (possibly)...circumcision.

Reference	Comments
Genesis 17:1-14	"For the generations to come every male among you who is eight days old must be circumcised..."
Isa iah 44:3	"I will pour out my Spirit on your offspring..."
Joel 2:28/29	"I will pour out my Spirit in those days."
Leviticus 16:4, Leviticus 16:24	Ceremonial washings
Ezekiel 36:25	"I will sprinkle clean water on you, and you will be clean..."
Psalms 51:1-3	"Wash away all my iniquity and cleanse me from my sin..."

Whether circumcision should be viewed as an Old Testament form of baptism is a theological choice primarily dictated by whether one believes in infant baptism or not. Those in favor of the circumcision/baptism linkage argue that, just as circumcision marked a child in the Old Testament as being part of the covenant of Abraham, so infant baptism in the Christian sense marks a child as being part of the new covenant of Jesus Christ. John Calvin, one of the founders of the Reformed Church, comments:

> We have, therefore, a spiritual promise given to the fathers in circumcision, similar to that which is given to us in baptism, since it figured to them both the forgiveness of sins and the mortification of the flesh...The only difference which remains is in the external ceremony, which is the least part of it, the chief part consisting in the promise

and the thing signified. **Hence we may conclude, that everything applicable to circumcision applies also to baptism, excepting always the difference in the visible ceremony**...For just as circumcision, which was a kind of badge to the Jews, assuring them that they were adopted as the people and family of God, was their first entrance into the Church, while they, in their turn, professed their allegiance to God, so now we are initiated by baptism, so as to be enrolled among his people, and at the same time swear unto his name. **Hence it is incontrovertible, that baptism has been substituted for circumcision, and performs the same office.** (*Institutes of the Christian Religion*, John Calvin, translated by Henry Beveridge[42])

The Roman Catholic Church takes a similar view, believing that baptism is the Christian equivalent of circumcision. Augustine commented on this several times in his writings:

Accordingly, when you ask why a Christian is not circumcised if Christ came not to destroy the law, but to fulfill it, my reply is, that a Christian is not circumcised precisely for this reason, that what was prefigured by circumcision is fulfilled in Christ. Circumcision was the type of the removal of our fleshly nature, which was fulfilled in the resurrection of Christ, and which the sacrament of baptism teaches us to look forward to in our own resurrection. The sacrament of the new life is not wholly discontinued, for our resurrection from the dead is still to come; but **this sacrament has been improved by the substitution of baptism for circumcision**, because now a pattern of the eternal life which is to come is afforded us in the resurrection of Christ, whereas formerly there was nothing of the kind. (*Reply to Faustus the Manichaean*, St. Augustine, A.D. 400, translated by Rev. Richard Stothert, M.A.; emphasis added[43])

"There is no doubt that to the ancient people of God circumcision stood in the place of baptism." (*The Three Books of Augustin, Bishop Of Hippo in Answer to the Letters of Petilian, the Donatist, Bishop of Cirta*, St. Augustine, translated by Rev. J.R. King[44])

In more modern terms, the Website "Catholic Answers" discusses "In Place of Circumcision":

---

42 Ages Software, 1996
43 *The Nicene and Post-Nicene Fathers First Series, Volume 4*, by Philip Schaff, editor
44 *Ibid*

Furthermore, Paul notes that baptism has replaced circumcision (Col. 2:11–12). In that passage, he refers to baptism as "the circumcision of Christ" and "the circumcision made without hands." Of course, usually only infants were circumcised under the Old Law; circumcision of adults was rare, since there were few converts to Judaism. If Paul meant to exclude infants, he would not have chosen circumcision as a parallel for baptism.

This comparison between who could receive baptism and circumcision is an appropriate one. In the Old Testament, if a man wanted to become a Jew, he had to believe in the God of Israel and be circumcised. In the New Testament, if one wants to become a Christian, one must believe in God and Jesus and be baptized. In the Old Testament, those born into Jewish households could be circumcised in anticipation of the Jewish faith in which they would be raised. Thus in the New Testament, those born in Christian households can be baptized in anticipation of the Christian faith in which they will be raised. The pattern is the same: If one is an adult, one must have faith before receiving the rite of membership; if one is a child too young to have faith, one may be given the rite of membership in the knowledge that one will be raised in the faith. This is the basis of Paul's reference to baptism as "the circumcision of Christ"—that is, the Christian equivalent of circumcision. (*Catholic Answers*[45])

The Baptist and Anabaptist (Mennonite, Amish) view on the idea of infant baptism replacing circumcision is, of course, somewhat different, and will be examined in due course.

---

[45] http://www.catholic.com/library/Infant_Baptism.asp

Chapter Thirteen - Baptism in the New Testament

John's baptism

John baptizing Jesus (Photo by Robert Jones)[46]

We are first introduced to the subject of Baptism in the New Testament through John the Baptist, an (unspecified) relative of Christ. John's baptism, typically practiced by full immersion in the Jordan River, is defined as "a baptism of repentance for the forgiveness of sins." This concept of a baptism of repentance, and for the forgiveness of sins later becomes an important element (although not, of course, the sole element) of Christian baptism.

Reference	Comments
Matthew 3:5 - 3:6	Baptized by him in the Jordan River.

46   From a stain glass window in the Cathedral of the Plains, Victoria, Kansas

Reference	Comments
Matthew 3:11	Baptism for repentance
Mark 1:4 - 1:8; Luke 3:3	"...a baptism of repentance for the forgiveness of sins."
Luke 3:1 - 3:18	Signs of true repentance
Luke 7:29 - 7:30	Effects of John's baptism
John 1:24 - 1:26	John's authority

John's baptism attracted enough attention in its time to have been recorded by Jewish historian Josephus 50 years later in his "Jewish Antiquities":

> Now some of the Jews thought that the destruction of Herod's army came from God, and that very justly, as a punishment of what he did against **John, that was called the Baptist**: for Herod slew him, who was a good man, and commanded the Jews to exercise virtue, both as to righteousness towards one another, and piety towards God, and so to come to baptism; for that the washing [with water] would be acceptable to him, if they made use of it, not in order to the putting away [or the remission] of some sins [only], but for the purification of the body; supposing still that the soul was thoroughly purified beforehand by righteousness... (*Jewish Antiquities*, Josephus, Book 18, Chapter 5[47])

The baptism of Christ

Of course, John's baptism would have an especially important role in beginning the ministry of Jesus Christ on earth. Jesus, although without sin, is baptized in the Jordan River by his relative John. The event is marked as especially important by the presence of all three persons of the Trinity - Christ as the incarnate Son of God, the voice of the Father, and the Holy Spirit "descending on him like a dove."

John also prepares us (without going into detail) that baptisms practiced by Christ in the future will be different from John's - John's baptism is by water, but Christ will baptize by fire.

Reference	Comments
Matt 3:11 - 3:17	"He will baptize you with the Holy Spirit and with fire."
Mark 1:9 - 1:11	The Spirit descending on him like a dove

---

[47] *The Works of Josephus*, translated by William Whitson

Reference	Comments
Luke 3:21 - 3:22	All persons of the Trinity present at the baptism
John 1:29 - 1:34	The reason for John's baptism
John 3:22 - 3:26	John still baptizing after baptism of Jesus

"Baptism of our savior. In the River Jordan"[48]

It has long been a matter of debate among theologians as to why Christ needed to be baptized at all. After all, John's baptism was for the forgiveness of sins, and Christ was without sin. 13th century Catholic theologian Thomas Aquinas suggests two reasons for the baptism of Christ:

> P(3)-Q(38)-A(1) ...first, it was necessary for Christ to be baptized by John, **in order that He might sanctify baptism**...Secondly, that **Christ might be manifested**. Whence John himself says (John 1:31): "That He," i.e. Christ, "may be made manifest in Israel, therefore am I come baptizing with water." For he announced Christ to the crowds that gathered around him; which was thus done much more easily than if he had gone in search of each individual... (*Summa Theologica*, Thomas Aquinas, English Dominican Translation[49])

---

48 Library of Congress LC-DIG-pga-01471
49 Ages Software, Copyright 1997

The Jordan River today (Photo by Barbara Brim)

Baptism as practiced by the first Christians

The New Testament gives fascinating clues as to how Christ and the apostles viewed baptism. However, there is no "Handbook on Baptism" in the New Testament. We can only surmise the proper form and meaning of baptism based on various verses that mention the sacrament. The meaning of many of the verses referenced below would be disputed by numerous groups over the next 2,000 years, and remain in dispute today.

Reference	Comments
Christ and Baptism	
Matt 19:14	"Let the little children come to me..." - sometimes used to justify infant baptisms
Matt 28:18 - 28:20	The Great Commission – "Therefore go and make disciples of all nations, baptizing them..."
Mark 16:15 - 16:18	"Whoever believes and is baptized will be saved..." seems to infer that belief precedes baptism. Baptists view that this verse invalidates infant baptism.
John 3:1 - 3:8	"...no one can enter the kingdom of God unless he is born of water and the Spirit." is sometimes used to justify the view that water baptism is necessary for salvation

Reference	Comments
John 4:1 - 4:2	Jesus did not baptize
Pentecost	
Luke 24:49	Jesus talks about the coming Pentecost
Acts 1:4 - 1:5	"...in a few days you will be baptized with the Holy Spirit." – are water baptism and baptism by the Holy Spirit two separate things? Does one follow the other?
Acts 2:1 - 2:41	"All of them were filled with the Holy Spirit..."
Acts 2:38 – 2:39	"The promise is for you and your children..." -sometimes used to justify infant baptism
Baptism and the Apostles	
Acts 8:6 - 8:25	Baptism of Simon Magus; Acts 8:14/16 seems to indicate that baptism by the Holy Spirit can follow water baptism
Acts 8:26 - 8:40	Philip baptizes the eunuch
Acts 9:17 - 9:19	Saul receives the Holy Spirit from the laying on of hands by Ananias, and is then baptized
Acts 10:44 - 10:48	Gentiles receive Holy Spirit *before* water baptism
Acts 16:14 - 16:15; Acts 16:33; Acts 18:8, 1 Cor 1:16	Household baptisms – sometimes used to establish a scriptural basis for infant baptism
Acts 18:23 - Acts 18:28	Apollo – "...he knew only the baptism of John"
Acts 19:1 - 19:7	Paul baptizes followers of John the Baptist – "When Paul placed his hands on them, the Holy Spirit came on them..."
1 Cor 1:13 - 1:17	Paul came not to baptize but to preach
Meaning of Baptism	
Rom 6:3 - 6:4	"...all of us who were baptized into Christ Jesus were baptized into his death..."
1 Cor 12:13	"...we were all baptized by one Spirit into one body..."
Eph 4:4 - 4:6	"...one Lord, one faith, one baptism..."
Col 2:11-12	Paul seems to equate circumcision with baptism – sometimes used to establish a scriptural basis for infant baptism
Gal 3:26 - 3:28	"...all of you who were baptized into Christ have clothed yourselves with Christ"
Titus 3:5 - 3:6	"He saved us through the washing of rebirth and renewal by the Holy Spirit..."
1 Pet 3:18 - 3:22	Noah and family saved by water – "This water symbolizes baptism that now saves you also..."

Chapter Fourteen - Baptism in the pre-Nicene Early Church

Through a number of Early Church sources, we have detailed accounts both of the form of baptisms in the pre-Nicene Church, as well as the meaning and liturgy of baptism.

Meaning of baptism

The late 1st-century/early-second century Epistle of Barnabas (possibly written by the Apostle) contains the following description of Christian baptism:

> ...we indeed descend into the water full of sins and defilement, but come up, bearing fruit in our heart, having the fear [of God] and trust in Jesus in our spirit... (E*pistle of Barnabas, The Apostolic Fathers with Justin Martyr And Irenaeus*, translated by A. Cleveland Coxe, D.D.[50])

The Shepherd of Hermas, a popular book in the 2nd and 3rd century Eastern Church, describes the meaning of baptism as follows:

> ...before a man bears the name of the Son of God he is dead; but when he receives the seal he lays aside his deadness, and obtains life. The seal, then, is the water: they descend into the water dead, and they arise alive. (*Shepherd of Hermas*, translated by the Rev. F. Crombie, M.A., Similitude IX, Chapter 16[51])

Justin Martyr, in his c. 150 work "First Apology", describes baptism as follows:

> And for this [rite] we have learned from the apostles this reason. Since at our birth we were born without our own knowledge or choice, by our parents coming together, and were brought up in bad habits and wicked training; in order that we may not remain the children of necessity and of ignorance, **but may become the children of choice and knowledge, and may obtain in the water the remission of sins formerly committed, there is pronounced over him who chooses to be born again, and has repented of his sins,** the name of God the Father and Lord of the universe; he who leads to the laver the person that is to be washed calling him by this name alone. (*First Apology*,

---

50   *The Ante-Nicene Fathers Volume 1*, Edited by A. Roberts And J Donaldson
51   *The Ante-Nicene Fathers Volume 2*, Edited by A. Roberts and J Donaldson

Justin Martyr, *The Apostolic Fathers with Justin Martyr And Irenaeus*, translated by A. Cleveland Coxe, D.D.[52])

The c. 3rd-century "Constitutions of the Holy Apostles" discusses the seriousness of baptism and the potential consequences if a Christian continues to sin after being initiated into the faith through baptism:

> Beloved, be it known to **you that those who are baptized into the death of our Lord Jesus are obliged to go on no longer in sin**; for as those who are dead cannot work wickedness any longer, so those who are dead with Christ cannot practice wickedness. We do not therefore believe, brethren, that any one who has received the washing of life continues in the practice of the licentious acts of transgressors. **Now he who sins after his baptism, unless he repent and forsake his sins, shall be condemned to hell-fire.** (*Constitutions of the Holy Apostles, Fathers of the Third and Fourth Centuries*, translated by A. Cleveland Coxe, D.D., Book 2, Section 3[53])

By the fourth century, many people (including, possibly, the Emperor Constantine) put off getting baptized until they were near death, so that they could continue to live a sinful life!

The form of baptism

Events prior to a pre-Nicene baptism typically included a two to three year period of instruction into the Christian faith, and a period of fasting prior to the baptism.

> But before the baptism let the baptizer fast, and the baptized, and whatever others can; but thou shalt order the baptized to fast one or two days before. (*Teaching of the Twelve Apostles, Fathers of the Third and Fourth Centuries*, translated by A. Cleveland Coxe, D.D., Chapter 7[54])

Catechumens were expected to lead lives of purity, and to renounce Satan:

> But let him that is to be baptized be free from all iniquity; one that has left off to work sin, the friend of God, the enemy of the devil, the heir of God the Father, the fellow-heir of His Son; one that has re-

---

[52] *The Ante-Nicene Fathers Volume 1*, Edited by A. Roberts And J Donaldson
[53] *The Ante-Nicene Fathers Volume 7*, Edited by A. Roberts and J Donaldson
[54] *Ibid*

nounced Satan, and the demons, and Satan's deceits; chaste, pure, holy, beloved of God... (*Constitutions of the Holy Apostles*, *Fathers of the Third and Fourth Centuries*, translated by A. Cleveland Coxe, D.D., Chapter 7, Book 3, Section 18[55])

Baptisms were generally performed by church officials (bishops, presbyters, etc.) often in the period preceding Easter, or the period between Easter and Pentecost. The baptism itself included both an anointing with oil and/or ointment, as well as the dipping or immersion in water:

Thou therefore, O bishop, according to that type, shalt anoint the head of those that are to be baptized, whether they be men or women, with the holy oil, for a type of the spiritual baptism. After that, either thou, O bishop, or a presbyter that is under thee, shall in the solemn form name over them the Father, and Son, and Holy Spirit, and shall dip them in the water; and let a deacon receive the man, and a deaconess the woman, that so the conferring of this inviolable seal may take place with a becoming decency. And after that, let the bishop anoint those that are baptized with ointment. (*Constitutions of the Holy Apostles*, *Fathers of the Third and Fourth Centuries*, translated by A. Cleveland Coxe, D.D., Book 3, Section 16/17[56])

The meaning of the tri-part baptism (oil, water, ointment) is discussed:

But thou shalt beforehand anoint the person with the holy oil, and afterward baptize him with the water, and in the conclusion shall seal him with the ointment; that the anointing with oil may be the participation of the Holy Spirit, and the water the symbol of the death of Christ, and the ointment the seal of the covenants. (*Constitutions of the Holy Apostles*, Book 7, Chapter 22)

The Constitutions describe the meaning of the immersion and rising up out of the water:

This baptism, therefore, is given into the death of Jesus: the water is instead of the burial...the descent into the water the dying together with Christ; the ascent out of the water the rising again with Him.

---

[55] *Ibid*

[56] *Ibid*

(*Constitutions of the Holy Apostles*, translated by A. Cleveland Coxe, D.D., Book 3, Section 16/17[57])

In a passage from Hippolytus (c. 215 A.D.), it appears that whole families might have been baptized together, including their children. Hippolytus also seems to infer that full immersion is not a requirement for baptism:

> The stream shall flow through the baptismal tank or pour into it from above when there is no scarcity of water; but if there is a scarcity, whether constant or sudden, then use whatever water you can find. They shall remove their clothing. And first baptizes the little ones; if they can speak for themselves, they shall do so; if not, their parents or other relatives shall speak for them. (*The Apostolic Tradition*, Hippolytus, translated by Burton Scott Easton[58]).

The liturgy of baptism

Hippolytus also preserves an early baptismal creed in his writings. Similarities to the Apostles Creed are to be expected, as the Apostles Creed probably started out as a baptismal creed:

> When the person being baptized goes down into the water, he who baptizes him, putting his hand on him, shall say: "Do you believe in God, the Father Almighty?" And the person being baptized shall say: "I believe." Then holding his hand on his head, he shall baptize him once. And then he shall say: "Do you believe in Christ Jesus, the Son of God, who was born of the Virgin Mary, and was crucified under Pontius Pilate, and was dead and buried, and rose again the third day, alive from the dead, and ascended into heaven, and sat at the right hand of the Father, and will come to judge the living and the dead?" And when he says: "I believe," he is baptized again. And again he shall say: "Do you believe in the Holy Spirit, in the holy church, and the resurrection of the body?" The person being baptized shall say: "I believe," and then he is baptized a third time. (*A Baptismal Confession*, Third Century, Hippolytus[59])

Some baptismal creeds included, in addition to the affirmation of Christ as savior, the renunciation of Satan:

---

[57] *Ibid*
[58] http://www.chronicon.net/
[59] *Creeds of the Church*, Ages Software

I renounce Satan, and his works, and his pomps, and his worships, and his angels, and his inventions, and all things that are under him. (*Constitutions of the Holy Apostles*, translated by A. Cleveland Coxe, D.D., Book 7, Section 3[60])

---

[60] *The Ante-Nicene Fathers Volume 7*, Edited by A. Roberts and J Donaldson

Chapter Fifteen - The baptism of Constantine

Constantine is sometimes referred to as the "Savior of Christianity", because prior to his conversion, Christianity was still a persecuted religion in the Roman Empire. As late as 303 A.D., the Emperor Diocletian launched a massive persecution campaign against Christians. With the conversion of Constantine in 312 A.D., Christianity became not only respectable, but also ascendant.

In 312 A.D., Constantine marched on Rome, in an attempt to take over control of the Western Empire. Arrayed against him were the forces of Maxentius, four times as strong. Constantine's battlefield conversion is described by Ecclesiastical Historian Eusebius, in his 4th-century "The Life of the Blessed Emperor Constantine":

> HOW, WHILE HE WAS PRAYING, GOD SENT HIM A VISION OF A CROSS OF LIGHT IN THE HEAVENS AT MID-DAY, WITH AN INSCRIPTION ADMONISHING HIM TO CONQUER BY THAT.
>
> ACCORDINGLY he called on him with earnest prayer and supplications that he would reveal to him who he was, and stretch forth his right hand to help him in his present difficulties. And while he was thus praying with fervent entreaty, a most marvelous sign appeared to him from heaven, the account of which it might have been hard to believe had it been related by any other person...He said that about noon, when the day was already beginning to decline, he saw with his own eyes the trophy of a cross of light in the heavens, above the sun, and bearing the inscription, **CONQUER BY THIS. At this sight he himself was struck with amazement, and his whole army also**, which followed him on this expedition, and witnessed the miracle. (*The Life of the Blessed Emperor Constantine*, Eusebius, translated by Ernest Cushing Richardson, Phd.; emphasis added[61])

After having a similar vision of Christ in his sleep, Constantine makes "the priests of God his counselors", and:

> ...deemed it incumbent on him to honor the God who had appeared to him with all devotion. And after this, being fortified by well-grounded hopes in Him, he hastened to quench the threatening fire of

---

[61] *The Nicene and Post-Nicene Fathers, Second Series, Volume 1*, by Philip Schaff, editor

tyranny. (*The Life of the Blessed Emperor Constantine*, Eusebius, translated by Ernest Cushing Richardson, Phd.)

Constantine, of course, goes on to defeat Maxentius, to assume total control of the Western Empire.

Constantine becomes a strong supporter and learned student of Christianity. However, he delays being baptized – a common practice in the fourth century. While it was well known among the Bishops of Christianity that their enthusiastic emperor was not baptized, he was, to say the least, "assigned some slack":

> But the severe rules of discipline which the prudence of the bishops had instituted, were relaxed by the same prudence in favor of an Imperial proselyte, whom it was so important to allure, by every gentle condescension, into the pale of the church; and Constantine was permitted, at least by a tacit dispensation, to enjoy most of the privileges, before he had contracted any of the obligations, of a Christian. Instead of retiring from the congregation, when the voice of the deacon dismissed the profane multitude, he prayed with the faithful, disputed with the bishops, preached on the most sublime and intricate subjects of theology, celebrated with sacred rites the vigil of Easter, and publicly declared himself, not only a partaker, but, in some measure, a priest and hierophant of the Christian mysteries. (*The History of the Decline and Fall of the Roman Empire Vol. 2*, by Edward Gibbon[62])

It is not until near his death that Constantine agrees to be baptized. These "deathbed conversions" were common in the 4th century. When catechumens were baptized in the early church, they were expected to live pure and chaste lives from that point on. There was a temptation to hold off on Christian baptism with its demands for purity, until one was old, or even nearing death, to avoid a lifetime requirement of righteous living. Constantine seems to have been one Christian with those views!

Whatever the reason for the delay, Constantine did finally agree to be baptized in 337 A.D, shortly before his death. Surely, this was the most famous and significant baptism since Paul! It is described by Eusebius:

---

[62]   Ages Software, 1999

Being at length convinced that his life was drawing to a close, he felt the time was come at which he should seek purification from sins of his past career, firmly believing that whatever errors he had committed as a mortal man, his soul would be purified from them through the efficacy of the mystical words and the salutary waters of baptism...After this he proceeded as far as the suburbs of Nicomedia, and there, having summoned the bishops to meet him, addressed them in the following words:

"THE time is arrived which I have long hoped for, with an earnest desire and prayer that I might obtain the salvation of God. The hour is come in which I too may have the blessing of that seal which confers immortality; the hour in which I may receive the seal of salvation. I had thought to do this in the waters of the river Jordan, wherein our Savior, for our example, is recorded to have been baptized: but God, who knows what is expedient for us, is pleased that I should receive this blessing here..." (*The Life of the Blessed Emperor Constantine*, Eusebius, translated by Ernest Cushing Richardson, Phd.[63])

Constantine was then baptized "in the usual manner." Finally, Eusebius reports the profound significance of this baptism (a significance that still resounds to this very day):

> Thus was Constantine the first of all sovereigns who was regenerated and perfected in a church dedicated to the martyrs of Christ; thus gifted with the Divine seal of baptism... (*The Life of the Blessed Emperor Constantine*, Eusebius, translated by Ernest Cushing Richardson, Phd.[64])

The long reign of terror and persecution against Christians was over!

---

[63] *The Nicene and Post-Nicene Fathers, Second Series, Volume 1*, by Philip Schaff, editor

[64] *Ibid*

Chapter Sixteen - St. Augustine and the Donatist schism

More events significant to the history of Christian baptism were to occur throughout the end of the 4th century, and into the 5th. They involved two schismatic groups named the Donatists and Pelagians, and one Christian saint and theologian, St. Augustine of Hippo. Out of the battle between these two schismatic groups and the Catholic Church were to arise Augustinian tenets regarding baptism that are still followed by the Roman Catholic Church today:

- Baptisms are conferred by Christ, not by the priest or bishop doing the baptism. Therefore, baptisms conferred by impure or schismatic bishops could be accepted as "official."
- Baptisms are necessary for salvation
- Children are tainted with the "original sin" of Adam and Eve. Therefore, not only are infant baptisms allowable, but are necessary, in case of an untimely death.

Novatian

The roots of the Donatist schism, against which St. Augustine so eloquently argued in the late 4th/early 5th centuries, date back to an earlier era. In c. 250 A.D., Emperor Decius ordered the persecution of Christians. As a result of this persecution, the Bishop of Rome Fabianus was murdered, and Church Father Origen was jailed. Many Christians (including some priests and bishops) committed apostasy – denying Christ to save themselves from persecution. After the persecutions ebbed in 251 A.D., the question was asked "Should priests that committed apostasy be allowed back into the church?"

Roman churchman Novatian (c. 200–258 A.D.) argued against admitting those that committed apostasy back into the church. Novatian cited such New Testament verses as:

> Whoever acknowledges me before men, I will also acknowledge him before my Father in heaven. But whoever disowns me before men, I will disown him before my Father in heaven. (Matthew 10:32-33, NIV)

After losing the election to fill the vacant position of Bishop of Rome in 251 A.D., Novatian and his followers split away from the Catholic Church. By 254 A.D., however, when it was clear that Novatian was not receiving support from outside his circle of followers, many of the followers of Novatian had fled, or desired (re)entry into the Catholic Church.

A great debate was waged between Bishop (254-56 A.D.) Stephen of Rome, who argued that those baptized by Novatianists could be accepted into the Catholic Church without being rebaptized, and Cyprian of Carthage (c. 195–258 A.D.), who argued that baptisms given by schismatics were not real baptisms at all. The following quote from Cyprian is representative of his views on the subject:

> You have written to me, dearest brother, wishing that the impression of my mind should be signified to you, as to what I think concerning the baptism of heretics; who, placed without, and established outside the Church, arrogate to themselves a matter neither within their right nor their power. This baptism we cannot consider as valid or legitimate, since it is manifestly unlawful among them... (*Epistle 72 - To Jubaianus, Concerning The Baptism Of Heretics*, Cyprian, translated by the Rev. Ernest Wallis, Ph.D.[65])

Stephen, whose view ultimately prevailed (and was later strongly seconded by Augustine), noted that baptism belongs to Christ, not the church, and the standing of the baptizer is not the relevant issue.

The causes of Novatian (against apostasy) and Cyprian (against validating baptisms by schismatics) would later be taken up by a group called the Donatists.

The Donatists

The situation in the early fourth century was similar to that of 50 years earlier. Emperor Diocletian had ordered the persecution of Christians throughout the empire (303 – 306 A.D.), and many Christians (including some bishops and priests) had committed apostasy. After Constantine came into power, the question of the mid-third

---

[65] *The Ante-Nicene Fathers Volume 5*, Edited by A. Roberts and J Donaldson

century remained – what to do about those that had committed apostasy? The situation boiled over at Carthage in 311 A.D. when an archdeacon named Caecilianus was ordained by a bishop that was suspected of having committed apostasy during the Diocletian persecution. In retaliation, the Donatists set up a rival Bishop of Carthage (Majorinus in 311 A.D.; Donatus in 315 A.D.)

In time, the Donatists became a schismatic sect, claiming that they were the only true Christians. The Donatists refused to accept baptisms performed in the Catholic Church, claiming they were invalid:

> Whenever they [Donatists] acquired a proselyte, even from the distant provinces of the East, they carefully repeated the sacred rites of baptism and ordination; as they rejected the validity of those which he had already received from the hands of heretics or schismatics. Bishops, virgins, and even spotless infants, were subjected to the disgrace of a public penance, before they could be admitted to the communion of the Donatists. If they obtained possession of a church which had been used by their Catholic adversaries, they purified the unhallowed building with the same zealous care which a temple of idols might have required. They washed the pavement, scraped the walls, burnt the altar, which was commonly of wood, melted the consecrated plate, and cast the Holy Eucharist to the dogs, with every circumstance of ignominy which could provoke and perpetuate the animosity of religious factions. (*The History of the Decline and Fall of the Roman Empire Vol. 2*, by Edward Gibbon[66])

The Donatists also insisted that a baptism performed by an "impure" priest was not valid.

While Donatism was condemned at the Council of Arles in 314 A.D., it continued to flourish. Beginning in 393 A.D., St. Augustine, the great theologian of the early Catholic Church, turned his skills of eloquence and logic against the Donatists. Central to the debate was, once again, baptism. It has already been noted that the Donatists forced Catholic proselytes to be rebaptized. However, the Catholic Church did not force "reformed" Donatists that wished to (re)join the Catholic Church to be rebatized, following the logic of Bishop Stephen of Rome in 254 A.D. – baptism is of Christ, not of the baptizer.

---

[66] Ages Software, 1999

It was against this backdrop (and also against the later Pelagian schism) that Augustine of Hippo began promulgating his theological views on baptism, which are still the standards of the Roman Catholic Church today.

One baptism

It is true that Christ's baptism is holy; and although it may exist among heretics or schismatics, yet it does not belong to the heresy or schism; and therefore even those who come from thence to the Catholic Church herself ought not to be baptized afresh.

And as the baptized person, if he depart from the unity of the Church, does not thereby lose the sacrament of baptism, so also he who is ordained, if he depart from the unity of the Church, does not lose the sacrament of conferring baptism.

So those, too, who in the sacrilege of schism depart from the communion of the Church, certainly retain the grace of baptism, which they received before their departure, seeing that, in case of their return, it is not again conferred on them whence it is proved, that what they had received while within the unity of the Church, they could not have lost in their separation.

...we act rightly who do not dare to repudiate God's sacraments, even when administered in schism. (*The Seven Books Of Augustin, Bishop Of Hippo, On Baptism, Against The Donatists*, St. Augustine, translated by Rev. J.R. King, M.A.[67])

On Cyprian's view of baptism in the third century

He [Cyprian] had therefore imperfect insight into the hidden mystery of the sacrament. (*The Seven Books Of Augustin, Bishop Of Hippo, On Baptism, Against The Donatists*, St. Augustine, translated by Rev. J.R. King, M.A.[68])

---

[67] *The Nicene and Post-Nicene Fathers, First Series, Volume* 4, by Philip Schaff, editor

[68] *Ibid*

Chapter Seventeen - St. Augustine and the Pelagian schism

While St. Augustine established for all time some important tenets of baptism in his battle with the Donatists, his theological conclusions that resulted from his battle with the Pelagians were even more significant and far reaching.

Pelagius (c. 354 A.D. - after 418) was a British Monk who was horrified by the seeming lack of piety and purity practiced by Christians in Rome c. 380 A.D. He felt that the laxness of Roman Christians grew partly from the prevailing doctrine of Grace, which stated that humans on their own are incapable of purity, and can only be saved by God's grace.

Pelagius and his followers (one student named Coelestius was especially influential) denied predestination, original sin, and the doctrine of Grace, maintaining the humans are not tainted by the sin of Adam and Eve, and that babies are born pure. As a result, humans have the free will to choose to live sinless lives. (In his somewhat confused theology, though, Pelagius still maintained that babies needed to be baptized.)

Augustine's response to the Pelagian heresy was vociferous and voluminous – Augustine wrote at least thirteen works and letters against Pelagius, and firmly entrenched in Catholic theology the doctrines of:

- Salvation through Grace
- Original Sin
- The necessity of baptism for salvation
- The damnation of unbaptized infants

It should be noted that tenets three and four above are seemingly inconsistent with the doctrine of predestination, of which Augustine was a proponent. A thousand years later, John Calvin (as we shall see) would argue against the **necessity** of infant baptism for this very reason.

Original Sin/necessity for infant baptism

...even if there were in men nothing but **original sin**, it would be sufficient for their condemnation...even that sin alone which was origin-
ally derived unto men not only excludes from the kingdom of God,
which infants are unable to enter (as they themselves allow), unless
they have received the grace of Christ before they die, but also alien-
ates from salvation and everlasting life, which cannot be anything else
than the kingdom of God, to which fellowship with Christ alone introduces us.

Hence men are on the one hand born in the flesh liable to sin and
death from the first Adam, and on the other hand are born again in
baptism associated with the righteousness and eternal life of the
second Adam...

For who would dare to say that Christ is not the Savior and Redeemer
of infants? But from what does He save them, if there is no malady of
original sin within them? From what does He redeem them, if through
their origin from the first man they are not sold under sin? Let there
be then no eternal salvation promised to infants out of our own opinion, without Christ's baptism; for none is promised in that Holy Scripture which is to be preferred to all human authority and opinion. (*A
Treatise On The Merits And Forgiveness Of Sins And On The Baptism
Of Infants*, St. Augustine, translated by Benjamin B. Warfield, D.D.[69])

Necessity of baptism for salvation

If, therefore, as so many and such divine witnesses agree, neither salvation nor eternal life can be hoped for by any man without baptism
and the Lord's body and blood, it is vain to promise these blessings to
infants without them. (*A Treatise On The Merits And Forgiveness Of
Sins And On The Baptism Of Infants*, St. Augustine, translated by Benjamin B. Warfield, D.D.[70])

Fate of infants that die before being baptized

So that infants, unless they pass into the number of believers through
the sacrament which was divinely instituted for this purpose, will un-
doubtedly remain in this darkness.

It may therefore be correctly affirmed, that such infants as quit the
body without being baptized will be involved in the mildest condem-

---

[69] *The Nicene and Post-Nicene Fathers First Series, Volume 5*, by Philip Schaff, edit-
or
[70] *Ibid*

nation of all..[71] (*A Treatise On The Merits And Forgiveness Of Sins And On The Baptism Of Infants*, St. Augustine, translated by Benjamin B. Warfield, D.D.[72])

---

[71] Even Augustine seemed a bit uncomfortable with the idea that infants that die unbaptized are damned to suffer in hell for eternity!

[72] *The Nicene and Post-Nicene Fathers First Series, Volume 5, by Philip Schaff, editor*

Chapter Eighteen - The Protestant Reformation

The basic views on baptism promulgated by St. Augustine in the late fourth and early fifth centuries remained the effective doctrine of the Roman Catholic Church for the next thousand years (with, perhaps, some refinement by Thomas Aquinas in his *Summa Theologica*). Only with the coming of the Protestant Reformation in the 16th century would millennium-old doctrines and theologies begin to be challenged, including:

- The necessity of baptism for salvation (challenged by the Reformed Church - John Calvin)
- The form of baptism - sprinkling vs. immersion (challenged by Baptists)
- Infant baptism (challenged by the Anabaptists & Baptists)
- Unbaptized infants that die are consigned to hell (challenged by Anabaptists, the Reformed Church)

Luther's views on baptism

Many people date the beginning of the Protestant Reformation to October 31, 1517, when Martin Luther tacked his 95 theses to the door of Wittenburg Castle. However, Luther strictly followed the status quo when it came to baptism – he supported infant baptism, and viewed that baptism was necessary to salvation:

> Baptism is no human trifle, but instituted by God Himself, moreover, that it is most solemnly and strictly commanded **that we must be baptized or we cannot be saved**, lest any one regard it as a trifling matter, like putting on a new red coat. (*Large Catechism*, Martin Luther, 1528, translated by F. Bente and W. H. T. Dau[73])

The more revolutionary views on baptism would come from the Reformed Church, the Anabaptists, and the Baptists.

---

[73] Ages Software, 1997

John Calvin and the Reformed Church

John Calvin[74]

John Calvin, one of the founders of the Reformed Church, and perhaps the greatest theologian since Thomas Aquinas, agreed with the Augustinian (and thus, Roman Catholic) views on baptism in several areas, including the idea that people should only be baptized once, and that the purity of the person conferring the baptism was irrelevant:

> We ought to consider that at whatever time we are baptized, **we are washed and purified once for the whole of life**. Wherefore, as often as we fall, we must recall the remembrance of our baptism, and thus fortify our minds, so as to feel certain and secure of the remission of sins. For though, when once administered, it seems to have passed, it is not abolished by subsequent sins.
>
> Moreover, if we have rightly determined that a sacrament is not to be estimated by the hand of him by whom it is administered, but is to be received as from the hand of God himself, from whom it undoubtedly

---

[74] Library of Congress LC-USZ62-72002

proceeded, we may hence infer **that its dignity neither gains nor loses by the administrator**. And, just as among men, when a letter has been sent, if the hand and seal is recognized, it is not of the least consequence who or what the messenger was; so it ought to be sufficient for us to recognize the hand and seal of our Lord in his sacraments, let the administrator be who he may. (*Institutes of the Christian Religion*, John Calvin, translated by Henry Beveridge[75])

John Calvin also agreed with Early Church Fathers such as Hippolytus that the form of baptism was not of consequence – both sprinkling and immersion are acceptable:

Whether the person baptized is to be wholly immersed, and that whether once or thrice, or whether he is only to be sprinkled with water, is not of the least consequence: churches should be at liberty to adopt either, according to the diversity of climates, although it is evident that the term baptize means to immerse, and that this was the form used by the primitive Church. (*Institutes of the Christian Religion*, John Calvin, translated by Henry Beveridge[76])

However, Calvin did not believe that baptism was either the cause of salvation, nor was it necessary to salvation:

Peter also says that "baptism also doth now save us" (1 Peter 3:21). For he did not mean to intimate that our ablution and salvation are perfected by water, or that water possesses in itself the virtue of purifying, regenerating, and renewing; nor does he mean that it is the cause of salvation, but only that the knowledge and certainty of such gifts are perceived in this sacrament.

...**we must not deem baptism so necessary as to suppose that everyone who has lost the opportunity of obtaining it has forthwith perished**. By assenting to their fiction, we should condemn all, without exception, whom any accident may have prevented from procuring baptism, how much soever they may have been endued with the faith by which Christ himself is possessed. (*Institutes of the Christian Religion*, John Calvin, translated by Henry Beveridge[77])

---

[75] Sage Software, 1996
[76] Ibid
[77] Ibid

Calvin viewed that a primary goal of baptism, rather than to confer salvation, was to make a public profession of faith, and to join the Universal Church of believers:

> Baptism serves as our confession before men, inasmuch as it is a mark by which we openly declare that we wish to be ranked among the people of God, by which we testify that we concur with all Christians in the worship of one God, and in one religion; by which, in short, we publicly assert our faith, so that not only do our hearts breathe, but our tongues also, and all the members of our body, in every way they can, proclaim the praise of God. (*Institutes of the Christian Religion*, John Calvin, translated by Henry Beveridge[78])

John Calvin also strongly believed in the practice of infant baptism:

> If, by baptism, Christ intends to attest the ablution by which he cleanses his Church, it would seem not equitable to deny this attestation to infants, who are justly deemed part of the Church, seeing they are called heirs of the heavenly kingdom. (*Institutes of the Christian Religion*, John Calvin, translated by Henry Beveridge[79])

While John Calvin was in favor of the practice of infant baptism, in a significant departure from Roman Catholic doctrine, he stated that unbaptized infants that die prematurely could still be saved. How? - through the doctrine of predestination. If, before the beginning of the world, God had pre-ordained that an infant was to be saved, the lack of baptism in the infant's temporal life would not be an inhibitor to salvation. As was noted earlier in this work, Augustine also believed in predestination, but did not apply the doctrine to infant baptism. It could be said that John Calvin took the theology of predestination to its logical conclusion with infant baptism.

> Our children, before they are born, God declares that he adopts for his own when he promises that he will be a God to us, and to our seed after us. In this promise their salvation is included. None will dare to offer such an insult to God as to deny that he is able to give effect to his promise. **How much evil has been caused by the dogma, in expounded, that baptism is necessary to salvation**, few perceive, and therefore think caution the less necessary... that children who happen to depart this life before an opportunity of immersing them in water,

---

[78] Ibid
[79] Ibid

are not excluded from the kingdom of heaven. (*Institutes of the Christian Religion*, John Calvin, translated by Henry Beveridge[80])

Westminster Confession

John Calvin's (and, it should be noted, Ulrich Zwingli's) views on baptism were to later be strongly echoed in the 1649 Westminster Confession, as the following excerpts demonstrate:

> 28:1 Baptism is a sacrament of the New Testament, ordained by Jesus Christ (Mat 28:19), not only for the solemn admission of the party baptized into the visible Church (1 Cor 12:13); but also, to be unto him a sign and seal of the covenant of grace (Rom 4:11 with Col 2:11, 12), of his ingrafting into Christ (Rom 6:5; Gal 3:27), of regeneration (Titus 3:5), of remission of sins (Mark 1:4), and of his giving up unto God through Jesus Christ, to walk in newness of life (Rom 6:3, 4). Which sacrament is, by Christ's own appointment, to be continued in His Church until the end of the world (Matt 28:19, 20).
>
> 28:3 Dipping of the person into the water is not necessary: but Baptism is rightly administered by pouring or sprinkling water upon the person (Mark 7:4; Acts 2:41; 16:33; Heb 9:10, 19-22).
>
> 28:4 Not only those that do actually profess faith in and obedience unto Christ (Mark 16:15, 16; Acts 8:37, 38), but also the infants of one or both believing parents, are to be baptized (Gen 17:7, 9 with Gal 3:9, 14, and Col 2:11, 12, and Acts 2:38, 39, and Rom 4:11, 12; Matt 28:19; Mark 10:13-16; Luke 18:15; 1 Cor 7:14).
>
> 28:5 Although it be a great sin to contemn or neglect this ordinance (Luke 7:30 with Ex 4:24-26), yet grace and salvation are not so inseparably annexed unto it, as that no person can be regenerated or saved without it (Acts 10:2, 4, 22, 31, 45, 47; Rom 4:11); or, that all that are baptized are undoubtedly regenerated (Acts 8:13, 23).
>
> 28:7 The sacrament of Baptism is but once to be administered unto any person (Titus 3:5). (Westminster Confession, Chapter XXVIII)

The Anabaptists

The emergence of the Anabaptist movement rose out of the belief that there is no Biblical basis for infant baptism. The Anabaptists broke away from the Reformed Church of Swiss Reformer Ulrich Zwingli (1484-1531). In Zwingli's Zurich, infant baptism was used by

---

[80] Ibid

the secular government for tax registration, and it was from the city government of Zurich that Zwingli had his authority. The Anabaptists broke away when Zwingli refused to refute this practice.

On January 21, 1525, an event occurred in Zurich which still reverberates today, almost 500 years later. Several of Zwingli's students (including Conrad Grebel, Feliz Manz and Georg Blaurock) "illegally" rebaptized each other, viewing that their baptism as infants was invalid. While the Anabaptist movement had other views that distinguished it from the Reformed Church of Zwingli (separation of church and state, for one), this event (and the theology that it stood for) became so strongly associated with the group that their very name reflects it:

> The name Anabaptists which is now applied to them, has but lately come into use, deriving its matter from the matter of holy baptism, concerning which their views differ from those of all, so-called, Christendom. (*Martyrs Mirror*, by Thieleman J. van Braght, 1660[81])

The Anabaptist view on infant baptism is summarized in the following passage:

> Of Holy Baptism, and why we have preferred it to all other articles, in our history: "...Because it is the only sign and proof of incorporation into the visible Christian church, without which no one, whoever he be, or whatever he may profess, or how separated and pious a life he may lead, can be recognized as a true member of the Christian Church...Because it is, beyond contradiction, the only article on account of which others call us Anabaptists. For, since all other so-called Christians have, yet without true foundation, this in common that they baptize infants; **while with us the baptism only which is accompanied by faith and a penitent life, according to the word of God, is administered to adults**; it follows, that with us such persons are baptized who have received baptism in their childhood, without faith and repentance; who, when they believe and repent, are again, or at least truly baptized with us; because with us their previous baptism, being without true foundation, and without the word of God, is not considered baptism at all. (*Martyrs Mirror*, by Thieleman J. van Braght, 1660[82])

---

[81] Herald Press, 1992
[82] Ibid

Compared to the Lutheran and Reformed Church successors, the Anabaptists are a comparably small group today, with the Amish, Mennonites, and Hutterites comprising about 1,000,000 members worldwide. However, while there is no unbroken line of succession between the Anabaptists and the modern day Baptists (over 32,000,000 strong in the U.S.A.), there is certainly great doctrinal similarity. The Anabaptists may be considered the spiritual predecessors of the American Baptist movement.

Amish farmer in Lancaster County, PA (1987) (Photo by Robert Jones)

The Baptists

> The true constitution of the Church is of a new creature baptized into the Father, the Son, and the Holy Ghost: **The false constitution is of infants baptized**: we profess therefore that all those Churches that baptize infants are of the same false constitution: and all those Churches that baptize the new creature, those that are made Disciples by teaching, men confessing their faith and their sins, are of one true constitution... (*The Character of the Beast*, John Smyth, 1609[83])

The Baptist movement grew out of the Puritan/Separatist movements in England in the 17th century. The Puritans, generally Calvinists, wanted the Church of England to be more democratic in its govern-

---

[83] *The Baptists: A People Who Gathered "To Walk in All His Ways."*, Christian History, Issue 6, April 1985

mental structure, and less Catholic in its trappings, liturgy, and rituals. (The Puritans were members of the Church of England, who wished to "purify" the church from within.) The Separatists were more radical, desiring a complete break from the Church of England. Out of the Separatist movement came both the Pilgrims and the Baptists.

The man often cited as the "first" Baptist is John Smyth (1570–1612), a former Anglican priest that became, in succession, a Puritan, a Separatist, and finally, a Baptist. In 1608, John Smyth (with the help of Thomas Helwys (?–1616)) took a group of Separatist followers to Amsterdam. During this period, Mennonites, descendents of the 16th century Anabaptists influenced Smyth and his followers.

In 1609, in a scene somewhat reminiscent of the Anabaptist "re-baptizing" ceremony in Zurich 90 years before, Smyth re-baptized himself and 40 followers, reasoning that their baptism as infants were invalid. What was soon to become the Baptist Church had begun.

In 1644, a group of Calvinist Particular Baptists published their "London Confession", affirming believers' baptism as a key tenet:

> **Baptism is an ordinance of the New Testament, given by Christ, to be dispersed only upon persons professing faith.** The way and manner of dispensing this Ordinance the Scripture holds to be **dipping or plunging the whole body under water.** - *The London Confession, 1644; emphasis added*[84])

As noted in the bold text above, both believers' baptism, and baptism by immersion were central to their beliefs - a final separation from Augustinian views on baptism.

---

[84]   *The Baptists: A People Who Gathered "To Walk in All His Ways."* Christian History, Issue 6, April 1985

Chapter Nineteen - The Great Debate: Infant Baptism vs. Believers' Baptism

Perhaps the greatest continuing debate regarding baptism in the Universal Church is infant baptism vs. believers' baptism. In this section, we examine some of the basic arguments on both sides of the issue.

In general, those that believe in believers' baptism outline the following arguments in favor of their position:

- Infant baptism is not mentioned in the Bible, the sole authority for Christians
- Infant baptism doesn't show up in the writings of the Early Church Fathers until Irenaeus c. 182/88, over 100 years after the writing of the Gospels
- Christ states in Mark 16:16 that "Whoever **believes** and is baptized will be saved, but whoever does not believe will be condemned" (NIV), indicating that belief must precede baptism

Infant baptism is not mentioned in the Bible, the sole authority for Christians

Perhaps the strongest argument against infant baptism is that it is nowhere explicitly mentioned in the New Testament:

> The word of God, in all its length and breadth, contains not a syllable of authority for infant baptism, in the form of command, of precept, of permission, of example, or in any other form whatever. In that sacred book not one word in relation to it, is anywhere uttered. (*Evils of Infant Baptism*, by R.B.C. Howell, 1851[85])

Those in favor of infant baptism typically refer to:

- The New Testament refers to household baptisms

> Everyone must now see that paedobaptism, which receives such strong support from Scripture, is by no means of human invention. Nor is there anything plausible in the objection, that we nowhere read of even one infant having been baptized by the hands of the apostles.

---

[85] Ages Software, 1997

For although this is not expressly narrated by the Evangelists, yet as they are not expressly excluded when mention is made of any baptized family (Acts 16:15, 32), what man of sense will argue from this that they were not baptized? (*Institutes of the Christian Religion*, John Calvin, translated by Henry Beveridge[86])

- In Luke 18:16, Christ states "Let the little children come to me, and do not hinder them, for the kingdom of God belongs to such as these." (NIV)

For we must not lightly overlook the fact, that our Savior, in ordering little children to be brought to him, adds the reason, "of such is the kingdom of heaven"...If it is right that children should be brought to Christ, why should they not be admitted to baptism, the symbol of our communion and fellowship with Christ? If the kingdom of heaven is theirs, why should they be denied the sign by which access, as it were, is opened to the Church, that being admitted into it they may be enrolled among the heirs of the heavenly kingdom? (*Institutes of the Christian Religion*, John Calvin, translated by Henry Beveridge[87])

- Acts 2:38-39 seems to connect baptism with children:

Peter replied, "Repent and be baptized, every one of you, in the name of Jesus Christ for the forgiveness of your sins. And you will receive the gift of the Holy Spirit. The promise is for you and your children and for all who are far off--for all whom the Lord our God will call." (Acts 2:38-39, NIV)

Church Tradition

A standard argument in favor of infant baptism is that the Early Church Fathers, including Origen, Augustine, and Hippolytus almost universally accepted it:

Both in the East and in the West the practice of baptizing infants is considered a rule of immemorial tradition. Origen, and later St. Augustine, considered it a "tradition received from the Apostles." When the first direct evidence of infant Baptism appears in the second century, it is never presented as an innovation. St. Irenaeus, in particular, considers it a matter of course that the baptized should include "infants and small children" as well as adolescents, young adults and older people. The oldest known ritual, describing at the start of the

---

[86] Sage Software, 1996

[87] Ibid

third century the Apostolic Tradition, contains the following rule: "First baptize the children. Those of them who can speak for themselves should do so. The parents or someone of their family should speak for the others." (*Instruction On Infant Baptism*, by the Sacred Congregation for the Doctrine of the Faith - Approved by His Holiness Pope John Paul II, October 20, 1980[88])

The argument against this position usually points out that there is no record of infant baptism in the church until a possible reference by Irenaeus late in the second century (c. 182/88), 100+ years after the Synoptic Gospels were written.

> Not till so late a period as — at least certainly not earlier than — Irenaeus appears a trace of infant baptism. That it first became recognized as an apostolic tradition in the course of the third century is evidence rather against, than for the admission of its apostolic origin, especially since, in the spirit of the age when Christianity appeared, there were many elements which must have been favorable to the introduction of infant baptism... (*Evils of Infant Baptism*, by R.B.C. Howell, 1851[89])

It should be noted also that the passage from Irenaeus mentioned by the Sacred Congregation for the Doctrine of the Faith above does not actually mention infant baptism by name:

> For He came to save all through means of Himself — all, I say, who through Him are born again to God — infants, and children, and boys, and youths, and old men. He therefore passed through every age, becoming an infant for infants, thus sanctifying infants; a child for children, thus sanctifying those who are of this age, being at the same time made to them an example of piety, righteousness, and submission; a youth for youths, becoming an example to youths, and thus sanctifying them for the Lord... (*Against Heresies*, Irenaeus, c. 180 A.D., *The Apostolic Fathers With Justin Martyr And Irenaeus*, translated by A. Cleveland Coxe, D.D.[90])

John Calvin weighs in on the topic of whether there was a long period of time between the writing of the Gospels, and the general acceptance of infant baptism by the Church Fathers:

---

[88] http://www.ewtn.com/library/CURIA/CDFINFAN.htm (and many others)
[89] Ages Software, 1997
[90] *The Ante-Nicene Fathers Volume 1*, Edited by A. Roberts and J Donaldson

The assertion which they [the Anabaptists] disseminate among the common people, that a long series of years elapsed after the resurrection of Christ, during which paedobaptism was unknown, is a shameful falsehood, since there is no writer, however ancient, who does not trace its origin to the days of the apostles. (*Institutes of the Christian Religion*, John Calvin, translated by Henry Beveridge[91])

Mark 16:16 – belief precedes baptism

A key point in the arsenal of those who believe in believerss baptism is the fact that Christ states in Mark 16:16 that "Whoever **believes** and is baptized will be saved, but whoever does not believe will be condemned" (NIV). This would seem to set an order of belief first, then baptism:

Those alone, who believe the gospel, they are required to baptize. The persons to be baptized are minutely described. They are believers. Believers therefore, and believers only, are to be baptized. A law to baptize believers is necessarily confined in its administration to believers. It embraces no others. To baptize any others is a violation of the law. It is unlawful. It is prohibited. Infants are not believers. (*Evils of Infant Baptism*, by R.B.C. Howell, 1851[92])

John Smyth, perhaps the first Baptist, viewed that baptism of the Spirit is required for a baptism to be valid (a view which would later become a key part of 20th century Pentecostalism):

For baptism is not washing with water: but it is the baptism of the Spirit, the confession of the mouth, and the washing with water: how then can any man without great folly wash with water which is the least and last of baptism, one that is not baptized with the Spirit, and cannot confess with the mouth: or how is it baptism if one be so washed: Now that an infant cannot be baptized with the Spirit is plain, 1 Pet. 3:21. where the Apostle saith that the baptism of the Spirit is the question of a good conscience unto God, and Heb. 10:22. where the baptism which is inward is called the sprinkling of the heart from an evil conscience: seeing therefore infants neither have an evil conscience, nor the question of a good conscience, nor the purging of the heart, for all these are proper to actual sinners: hence it followeth

---

91   Sage Software, 1996
92   Ages Software, 1997

that infants baptism is folly and nothing. (*The Character of the Beast*, John Smyth, 1609[93])

John Calvin viewed that the Mark 16:16 passage regarding the belief/baptism order was referring specifically to adults, and should not be applied to infants:

Whosoever believeth and is baptized, shall be saved. Is there one syllable about infants in the whole discourse? What, then, is the form of argument with which they assail us? Those who are of adult age are to be instructed and brought to the faith before being baptized, and therefore it is unlawful to make baptism common to infants. They cannot, at the very utmost, prove any other thing out of this passage, than that the gospel must be preached to those who are capable of hearing it before they are baptized; for of such only the passage speaks. (*Institutes of the Christian Religion*, John Calvin, translated by Henry Beveridge[94])

The debate, of course, continues to rage to this day.

Infant baptism in 2009 (Photo by Robert Jones)

---

93   *The Baptists: A People Who Gathered "To Walk in All His Ways."*, Christian History, Issue 6, April 1985

94   Sage Software, 1996

Appendix: "John's Baptism" - Influenced by Essene thought?

We've examined baptism in this book through the lens of the Old Testament and New Testament, but what about the period between the Testaments? Since baptism isn't mentioned explicitly in the Old Testament, where did John the Baptist come up with the idea of "baptism for the remission of sins"? Did such a concept exist in the latter part of the "Before Christ" period? Could John the Baptist have been influenced by a theology that developed between the Testaments??

Entrance to Cave 4 in the hills above Qumran[95]

Beginning in 1947, a massive treasure trove of ancient documents were found in caves above an ancient site known as Qumran, in the

---

[95]   Library of Congress LC-DIG-matpc-13012

Judean desert. Collectively, these documents are known as the Dead Sea Scrolls. Included in the over 800 scrolls discovered (the bulk of which range in date from about 150 B.C. to 68 A.D.) are several texts that can be described as the "constitution" (*Community Rule, Damascus Document, Messianic Rule*), or set of rules of a Jewish religious group.

The most prominent theory regarding the origins of these Scrolls is that they were the library of a Jewish religious group known as the Essenes[96]. In this view, the Essenes were a monastic-like group that lived in the Judean desert at Qumran (and perhaps other places, too). It is to the Essenes that we'll look as a possible precursor of "John's Baptism".

One of the more enigmatic figures in the New Testament is John the Baptist. First, we're told that John lived in the desert "until he appeared publicly to Israel":

> And the child grew and became strong in spirit; and he lived in the desert until he appeared publicly to Israel. (Luke 1:80, NIV)

Once he began his ministry, he preached a "baptism of repentance for the forgiveness of sins":

> And so John came, baptizing in the desert region and preaching a baptism of repentance for the forgiveness of sins. (Mark 1:4, NIV)

John's baptism attracted enough attention in its time to have been recorded by Jewish historian Josephus 50 years later in his *Jewish Antiquities*. Note the emphasis Josephus puts on the "remission of sins" aspect of the baptism.

> Now some of the Jews thought that the destruction of Herod's army came from God, and that very justly, as a punishment of what he did against John, that was called the Baptist: for Herod slew him, who was a good man, and commanded the Jews to exercise virtue, both as to righteousness towards one another, and piety towards God, and so to come to baptism; **for that the washing [with water] would be accept-**

---

[96] Another prominent theory is that the Dead Sea Scrolls are the library of the Temple, removed from Jerusalem and hid as the forces of Titus closed in on the city

able to him, if they made use of it, not in order to the putting away [or the remission] of some sins [only], but for the purification of the body; supposing still that the soul was thoroughly purified beforehand by righteousness... (*Jewish Antiquities*, Josephus , Book 18, Chapter 5, emphasis added[97])

Could John the Baptist have been raised an Essene – in the desert – at Qumran? Certainly, the Essenes attached a lot of importance to water purification. Qumran (if, indeed, it was the Essene capitol), had an elaborate system of cisterns, and five ritual baths. And both 1ˢᵗ century secular sources, and the *Community Rule* discuss the importance of water purification:

He shall be cleansed from all his sins by the spirit of holiness uniting him to His truth, and his iniquity shall be expiated by the spirit of uprightness and humility. **And when his flesh is sprinkled with purifying water and sanctified by cleansing water, it shall be made clean by the humble submission of his soul to all the precepts of God**. (*Community Rule*, Vermes translation; emphasis added[98])

They shall not enter the water to partake of the pure Meal of the men of holiness, for they shall not be cleansed unless they turn from their wickedness, for all who transgress His Word are unclean. (*Community Rule*, Vermes translation[99])

...and when they have clothed themselves in white veils, they then bathe their bodies in cold water. And after this purification is over... (*Jewish Wars*, Josephus , Book 2, Chapter 8[100])

Finally, both the *Community Rule*, and all four Gospels attach special significance to Isaiah 40:3. In the Gospel versions, John is explicitly identified as "A voice of one calling in the desert"

And when these become members of the Community in Israel according to these rules, they shall separate from the habitation of unjust men and shall go into the wilderness to prepare there the way of Him, as it is written, *Prepare in the wilderness the way of...make straight in*

---

[97] *The Works of Josephus*, translated by William Whitson
[98] *The Complete Dead Sea Scrolls in English*, Geza Vermes, Penguin Books, 1997
[99] *Ibid*
[100] *The Works of Josephus*, translated by William Whitson

the desert a path for our God. (*Community Rule*, Vermes translation[101])

In those days John the Baptist came, preaching in the Desert of Judea and saying, "Repent, for the kingdom of heaven is near." This is he who was spoken of through the prophet Isaiah: "A voice of one calling in the desert, 'Prepare the way for the Lord, make straight paths for him.'" (Matthew 3:1-3, NIV)

It should be noted that there are also two references in the Old Testament that connect water purification with remission of sins - Ezekiel 36:25, Psalms 51:1-3.

A modern day photo of Qumran (Photo by Barbara Brim)

---

[101] *The Complete Dead Sea Scrolls in English*, Geza Vermes, Penguin Books, 1997

Sources

Title	Author	Publisher	Year
A Treatise On The Merits And Forgiveness Of Sins And On The Baptism Of Infants - St. Augustine	Trans. by Peter Holmes, D.D., F.R.A.S., & Rev. Robert Ernest Wallis, Ph.D.	Ages Software	1997
Against Heresies - Irenaeus	Trans. by A. Cleveland Coxe, D.D.	Ages Software	1997
An Arthurian Reader	Ed. by John Matthews	The Aquarian Press	1988
Ante-Nicene Fathers Volume 1, The	Ed. by A. Roberts and J Donaldson	Ages Software	1997
Ante-Nicene Fathers Volume 7, The	Ed. by A. Roberts and J Donaldson	Ages Software	1997
Ante-Nicene Fathers Volume 8, The	Ed. by A. Roberts and J Donaldson	Ages Software	1997
Catholic Encyclopedia (http://www.newadvent.org/cathen/index.html)			
Commentary On The First Epistle To The Corinthians	John Calvin	Ages Software	1998
Complete Dead Sea Scrolls in English, The	Geza Vermes	Penguin Books	1997
Constitutions of the Holy Apostles	Edited, With Notes, by James Donaldson, D.D.	Ages Software	1997
Council of Trent, The Thirteenth Session, The canons and decrees of the sacred and ecumenical Council of Trent	Ed. and trans. J. Waterworth	Dolman	1848
Creeds Of The Church		Ages Software	1997
Decline and Fall of the Roman Empire	Edward Gibbon	Ages Software	1997

Title	Author	Publisher	Year
Disciplinary Decrees of the General Councils: Text, Translation and Commentary	H. J. Schroeder	B. Herder	1937
Ecclesiastical History - Eusebius	Trans. by Arthur Cushman McGiffert, Ph.D.	Ages Software	1997
Epistle 72 - To Jubaianus, Concerning The Baptism Of Heretics - Cyprian	Trans. by The Rev. Ernest Wallis, Ph.D	Ages Software	1997
Epistle of Barnabas	Trans. by A. Cleveland Coxe, D.D.	Ages Software	1997
Evils of Infant Baptism	R.B.C. Howell	Ages Software	1997
First Apology - Justin Martyr	Trans. by A. Cleveland Coxe, D.D.	Ages Software	1997
First Epistle of Clement to the Corinthians	Trans. by Archbishop Wake	Gramercy Books	1979
Holy Bible - New International Version		Zondervan Publishing House	1973
Institutes of the Christian Religion - John Calvin	Trans. by Henry Beveridge	Ages Software	1997
Instruction On Infant Baptism	By the Sacred Congregation for the Doctrine of the Faith	Approved by His Holiness Pope John Paul II	1980
Jewish Antiquities - Josephus	William Whiston, Translator	Ages Software	1997
Large Catechism - Martin Luther	Trans. by F. Bente and W. H. T. Dau	Ages Software	1997
Latin Works and Correspondence of Huldreich Zwingli, vol. 2, The		Heidelberg Press	1922
Letters of Martin Luther, The		Ages Software	1997
Lost Books of the Bible		Gramercy Books	1979
Martyr's Mirror	Thielman J. van Braght	Herald Press	1992
Nicene And Post-Nicene Fathers Second Series, Volume 4, The	Ed. Philip Schaff	Ages Software	1997

Title	Author	Publisher	Year
Nicene And Post-Nicene Fathers, First Series, Volume 10, The	Ed. Philip Schaff	Ages Software	1997
Nicene And Post-Nicene Fathers, First Series, Volume 14, The	Ed. Philip Schaff	Ages Software	1997
Nicene And Post-Nicene Fathers, First Series, Volume 2, The	Ed. Philip Schaff	Ages Software	1997
Nicene And Post-Nicene Fathers, Second Series, Volume 7, The	Ed. Philip Schaff	Ages Software	1997
Strong' Hebrew and Greek Dictionaries		Parson's Technology	1998
Symbolical Books of the Ev. Lutheran Church, The		Concordia Publishing House	1921
The Nicene and Post-Nicene Fathers First Series, Volume 4, The	Ed. Philip Schaff	Ages Software	1997
Tracts and Treatises John De Wycliffe D.D.		Blackburn and Pardon (Reprinted by Google Books)	1845

Weblinks

http://www.bombaxo.com/hippolytus.html
http://www.catholic.com/library/Infant_Baptism.asp
http://www.chronicon.net/
http://www.ewtn.com/library/CURIA/CDFINFAN.htm
http://www.newadvent.org/cathen/05572c.htm
http://www.newadvent.org/cathen/10006a.htm
http://www.newadvent.org/cathen/14424a.htm

About the Author

Robert C. Jones grew up in the Philadelphia, Pennsylvania area. In 1981, he moved to the Atlanta, Georgia area, where he received a B.S. in Computer Science at DeVry Institute of Technology. From 1984-2009, Robert worked for Hewlett-Packard as a computer consultant. He now works as an independent computer support and video services consultant.

Robert is an ordained elder in the Presbyterian Church. He has written and taught numerous adult Sunday School courses. He has also been active in choir ministries over the years, and has taught the Disciples Bible Study six times. He is the author of *A Brief History of Protestantism in the United States*, *A Brief History of the Sacraments: Baptism and Communion,* and *Meet the Apostles: Biblical and Legendary Accounts*.

Robert is President of the Kennesaw Historical Society, for whom he has written several books, including *The Law Heard 'Round the World - An Examination of the Kennesaw Gun Law and Its Effects on the Community*, *Retracing the Route of the General - Following in the Footsteps of the Andrews Raid*, and *Images of America: Kennesaw*.

Robert has also written several books on ghost towns in the Southwest, including in Death Valley, Nevada, Arizona, New Mexico, and Mojave National Preserve.

In 2005, Robert co-authored a business-oriented book entitled *Working Virtually: The Challenges of Virtual Teams*.

His interests include the Civil War, Medieval Monasteries, American railroads, ghost towns, hiking in Death Valley and the Mojave, and Biblical Archaeology.

Robert is available as a guest speaker in the Atlanta/North Georgia area (robertcjones@mindspring.com).

Cover: A stained-glass window at Mars Hill Presbyterian Church, Ac'